FAR ABOVE
RUBIES

BY

ISABEL HILL ELDER
(MERCH O LUNDAIN DERRI)

THE COVENANT PUBLISHING CO. LTD.
121, Low Etherley, Bishop Auckland, Co. Durham, DL14 0HA

2011

First edition 1957
Reprinted 2011

ISBN 978-085205-078-1

Printed by
THE COVENANT PUBLISHING COMPANY LIMITED
121, Low Etherley, Bishop Auckland,
Co. Durham, DL14 0HA
www.covpub.co.uk

Author of

CELT, DRUID & CULDEE
GEORGE OF LYDDA

DEDICATED

TO

BETTY-ROSE

'The best way to come to Truth is to examine things as they really are, and not to conclude they are, as we fancy of ourselves, or have been taught by others to imagine' (Locke).

'The Lord giveth the word: the women that publish the tidings are a great host' *(Psalm* 68:11, R.V.).

'Who can find a virtuous woman? for her price is far above rubies' *(Proverbs* 31:10).

FOREWORD
BY
THE HON. MRS. S. KAY SHUTTLEWORTH

THE author of this book, Mrs. I. Hill Elder, here presents a number of fine portraits of our ancestors. Let us read, mark, learn and inwardly digest that which teaches us a little more about the women who gave birth to the men who saved the situation for the people who Ruled-with-God—Isra-el.

CONTENTS

PREFACE

In the following biographical sketches of the more famous women of Israel an attempt has been made to supply what can hardly be said to exist already: a short historical work which might enable the reader of the Bible to realize that the women of both the Old and New Testaments were characters worthy of our highest esteem and very little removed in feeling and thought from ourselves. If this little work has any real value it is as a picture of manners and customs, a drama in which the personages are living characters and not mere historical names.

In the beginning woman was the equal of man in every respect; in patriarchal times she had an independence surpassing even today, and was entrusted with the administration of her husband's property as well as her own.

The women of heathen nations were the first to lose this independence which was retained by the women of Israel until the captivities. Upon the return of the Jewish captives from Babylon to Palestine a marked change is discernible; family life was never again the same. The women of both Houses of Israel had become degraded to the level of the women of their captors, and a woman was viewed by her husband as a mere chattel and his slave.

Perhaps no better illustration of the gradual decline in the status of women of ancient times could be found than that to be seen in the Gizeh Museum, near Cairo. Here there is displayed a long line of Egyptian monarchs in stone; at the end where the most ancient were placed the queen sat by the side of the king, of equal size and importance. A few centuries down the line the queen is found to be smaller than the king; progressing farther down the line the queen is found to be much smaller and to sit on a lower level than the king. Lastly, the queen is no longer carved out of a stone block, she is merely sketched in portraiture on the stool upon which the king sat or upon the arm of his throne.

This gradual change was reflected in every home, in every

relation of life, until her degradation was complete and the Israelites emerged from their captivities with the identical ideas of their captors as to the status and treatment of women. It is very significant that after Esther there is no Old Testament record of any woman of distinction in Israel. This is to be accounted for by the fact that the seventy Rabbis who translated the Scriptures from the Hebrew into Greek, known as the Septuagint, were influenced entirely by their contact with heathen peoples. These Rabbis believed that nothing good could be done or said by a woman, and in many instances their translation was influenced by heathen ideas. The social or moral status of any woman was of no account and the Talmud abounds with instances of her degradation. This idea of inferiority became so engrained that women, in spite of the uplift which Christianity brought, were convinced until a few decades ago that the woman should not aspire to be the equal of the man.

In her monumental work, *God's Word to Women,* Mrs. Katherine Bushnell has given the history of women from Eve onwards, and courageously challenges the misleading translation of many parts of the Scriptures which treat of women's place in the nation Israel.

When we come to the opening of the New Testament a marked change is discernible in the treatment of women, for our Lord began that uplift of women which has continued to the present day. He encouraged women to speak by addressing them and conversing with them in public, a liberty strictly forbidden by the Rabbis; even His disciples found it difficult to alter the views with which they were imbued, and though not daring to expostulate with Him on this point, they 'marvelled that He talked with the woman.'

St. Paul also found difficulty in changing over to our Lord's teaching regarding women, but gradually he came to give them their place in the Church and honoured them as his helpers.

Since then the all-too-slow upward movement in the status and dignity of women has gone on, and greatly accelerated in the past century, until today her ancient independence is restored; every career is open to her and no longer is she forced to occupy a position inferior in intelligence and governing ability. Before her lies a great and Divinely-appointed task in the part she has yet to play in leading the world in righteousness. In the words of Patience Strong:

'Lift up your voice and proclaim now your faith,
Lift up your eyes and behold:
The signs in the heavens, the glow in the East.
The wonder of things long foretold.

'You who are heirs of the promise of Israel
Be not dismayed nor cast down.
You of the Commonwealth, yours is the heritage.
Yours is the cross—and the crown.'

I. H. E.
BANGOR, CO. DOWN.

CHAPTER 1

SARAH *(Genesis* 17)

The great Mother of the Israel people, Sarah, the wife of Abraham, whose name was changed by Almighty God from the Chaldean 'Sarai' to the Hebrew 'Sarah' (signifying 'prince of the multitude'), was thereby marked for special blessing.

Abraham was to be a 'father of many nations,' while Sarah was to be a 'mother of nations' and, additionally, 'kings of people shall be of her.' Sarah's titles did not depend upon her position as wife of Abraham, the 'mighty prince;' upon her was bestowed the title of a female prince—Sarah.

It was not customary in ancient times for a wife to follow her husband in his wanderings; in this instance, however, when God called Abraham from Ur of the Chaldees, He willed both husband and wife to come out from idolatrous surroundings, and so we have Abraham saying to Abimelech, 'When God caused me to wander from my father's house. . .'[1]

Professor Flinders Petrie, English Egyptologist and archaeologist, has written on this subject, 'We have become so accustomed to the idea that women were always dependent in the East—as they are now under Mohammedism—that we need to open our eyes to a very different system which is shown us in the early history of the patriarchal age. Broadly, it may be said that our present system is the entire mixture of men and women in society,

---

[1] Author's Note.—An alternative rendering is: 'When God caused Sarah to wander with me.' See *The Samaritan Pentateuch and Modern Criticism* by the Rev. J. Inverach Munroe, M.A.

while men retain all the rights and property.

'The early ideal in the East was separate worlds of men and women, while women retained their own rights and all the property. . . . The first woman (aside from Eve) who appears as a personality in the Old Testament is Sarah, "the Chieftainess," as her name implies. Sar is the regular old term for a chief, still kept up in the East. . . . Her independent position is seen by her living in the palace of Pharaoh or in the Court of Abimelech, quite irrespective of Abraham. The attempt at explaining this away by later writers will not at all account for this independence, which was ignored in after ages. . . . Sarah had her independent residence at Mamre, and lived there, while Abraham lived at Beersheba, and it is said that he came to mourn for her, and to bury her. Her position, therefore, during her wanderings and in later life, was not by any means that of secluded dependence, but rather that of an independent head of the tribe, or tribal mother.'[2]

In the somewhat nomadic life upon which Abraham and his wife embarked, by God's command, Sarah's tent held the most important place when these temporary homes were pitched at the appointed resting places.

In his work, *Kinship and Marriage in Early Arabia,* Professor Robertson Smith states, 'Originally the tent belonged to the wife and her children.' The family home, therefore, belonged to the mother, while the husband occupied a small tent in the encampment. The unchanging East supplies us with many pictures of life in the days of the patriarchs; the following pen picture of the way of life of a Mongolian prince and his princess while on travel reveals very clearly the refinement and luxury maintained by people of affluence: 'The prince, accompanied by an immense retinue, was taking one of the fantastically long journeys in order to

---

[2] *Egypt and Israel.*

pay a vow at a distant Tibetan Lamasery. He was chief of a Kalmuk tribe whose home is in the more distant regions of Mongolia, among the Altai Mountains. . . . Our impression on entering the tent was that some Arabian Nights' fancy had materialized before our eyes. The ground was spread with beautifully-woven rugs, while inlaid boxes stood against the wooden trellis-work which formed the lower support of the felt tent. The smoke from a smouldering fire rose through the opening above which likewise served to admit light and air. On a low divan lay her sick child, and his mother sat beside him. At our entrance she rose with a stately grace and advanced to receive us. Her hair hung down in two long glistening plaits outlining the pure oval of her face and was gathered into jewelled sheaths forming part of the regal-head dress. Jade, gold and silver ornaments covered her breast, and a satin garment of sombre richness fell from her shoulders to her feet.

'A second tent held the servants, and was used as a kitchen. . . With amazing rapidity when an order is given to strike camp, the goats' and hair felts are rolled up, the inlaid boxes placed in their cases, and rugs strung into bales, the whole being secured to the pack saddles of the kneeling camels. The Princess herself rode her own splendid camel whose saddle was of most curious inlaid metal-work.'[3] In such surroundings Isaac was born and brought up, until, as with his father Abraham, he had his own tent and attendants.

Sarah, in giving her maid Hagar to Abraham, was but following the Hammurabi Law under which she lived, for it was quite permissible under that law to divorce a childless wife. Sarah did have some fear of divorcement and took the course permitted by law in obtaining a child for Abraham. Abraham accepted from his childless wife, Sarah, the gift of her maid Hagar as a wife of

---

[3] Mildred Cable and Francesca French, *Through Jade Gates*, p. 41.

inferior rank, in the hope that the latter would bear a child whom her mistress might adopt; the child, until adopted and formally declared free, is, like the mother, a slave and the property of the mistress, and can be sold or driven out as she pleases, the husband being helpless. That Abraham hoped that Sarah would adopt the child Ishmael, his son by Hagar, is clear from Abraham's prayer: 'O that Ishmael might live before Thee!;' and that Sarah did not adopt him is further evidence of her faith in the promise of Almighty God that she herself, though old and feeble, would yet bear a son (see *Hebrews* 11:11); hence, when Isaac was born Sarah demanded the expulsion of the slave and her son.

In the separation of Abraham and Sarah from idolatrous surroundings, and in the birth of Isaac, we see the first beginnings of a Christian family; we see the character of Sarah, especially, develop gradually under Divine grace, until she realizes that her household must be purified from all appearance of polygamy. The step she had to take was hard upon both Sarah and Hagar; both suffered for Sarah's fear of the lot of the childless wife and her impatience to obtain a child for Abraham by this quite lawful, though not Divinely-led, means. To Abraham was given the unpleasant task of 'sending away' Hagar and her son.

The 'obedience' of Sarah to Abraham is much stressed by certain groups of Christians to the total obscuration of Sarah's exalted position. 'As far as Abraham and Sarah are concerned, however, we are left in no doubt as to this relation and respect being mutual and reciprocal. God commanded Abraham to call Sarah by the very respectful name of "Princess".' [4] When Abraham was grieved that he was called upon to take this step, a Divine voice spoke to him, saying, 'In all that Sarah hath said unto thee, hearken unto her voice; for in Isaac shall thy seed be called.'

---

[4] Katharine Bushnell, *God's Word to Women*, para. 301.

Sarah is extolled for her excellences by both St. Peter and St. Paul, while Isaiah, in his exhortation to the nation Israel, bids the people 'look unto ... Sarah that bare you.' In the peoples, nations and kings who trace back to Sarah, we see the ample fulfilment of the promises made by Almighty God to Abraham and Sarah in those far-distant days while they dwelt at Hebron. Sarah said, 'God hath made me to laugh, so that all that hear will laugh with me.' Her son, Isaac, the child of promise, was given a name which signifies 'laughter.' The Dead Sea Scrolls discovered by shepherds in the Judean Desert in 1947 have aroused world-wide interest. The seventh of these scrolls gives striking testimony to the accuracy of the Scriptures and to the simple acknowledgment of Abraham to his wife, Sarah, 'Thou art a fair woman to look upon.' The description of Sarah as given in this Scroll is that of a woman of exquisite beauty with that rarity in the East, a pure white skin. Other points of physical beauty were noted and recorded so that today we have a quite accurate picture of the appearance of Sarah when she won the admiration of kings and princes and reigned as a great beauty among her contemporaries.

CHAPTER 2

REBEKAH *(Genesis* 24)

Upon the death of Sarah, Abraham set about the resolving of a most important matter—that of finding a wife for his son, Isaac, who would replace Sarah as 'tribal mother' and occupy Sarah's state tent. How this was accomplished is one of the most familiar episodes of the Bible.

It is noteworthy that when Abraham sent his steward, Eliezer, to choose a wife for Isaac from among his own relatives at Haran, the steward replied in astonishment, 'Peradventure the woman will not follow me,' so unusual was it in those days for a woman to leave her home upon marriage. Abraham did not wish Isaac to live in idolatrous surroundings and determined that the severance from such surroundings would be as complete as in his own case. It should be made clear, however, that Abraham's relatives at Haran were themselves, like Abraham, worshippers of the true God. The success of the mission of the God-fearing steward, Eliezer, first in meeting Rebekah, the beautiful daughter of Bethuel of Padan-Aram at the well, and then in gaining her favour ere she ran to her mother's house to announce his arrival, convinced the steward that Almighty God had answered his prayer, and that his long journey was to end in a betrothal which would be in complete compliance with Abraham's wishes. Laban, Rebekah's brother, came forth to welcome Eliezer and to bring him and his servants under his father's hospitable roof.

It is noteworthy, as further evidence of the importance of the wife and mother in patriarchal times, that Rebekah ran to her mother's house to report on her meeting with Abraham's steward, Eliezer.

With lavish hand Eliezer bestowed many and costly gifts upon Rebekah and her family as a means of revealing to them the affluence in which Rebekah would find herself as the wife of Isaac.

The consent of Rebekah's parents was not difficult to obtain, but it was Rebekah herself who was to decide this important matter; in her decisive, 'I will go,' we see that in those ancient times a woman was not coerced into marriage as she was in later times. The blessings called down upon Rebekah by her family, as she left her home, are remarkable and have had a wonderful fulfilment.

The imposing cavalcade set out to follow Eliezer: Rebekah, her nurse, Deborah, and her attendants all riding upon camels. Almost at the end of the long journey south, Rebekah, upon her first glimpse of her future husband, Isaac, walking towards the mounted company, 'lighted off the camel' and 'took a vail, and covered herself.' The original Hebrew word signifies a 'double' garment, a mantle, or shawl to cover up the dust of her travelling costume, probably embroidered on both sides, and the same as that mentioned in Deborah's song as being coveted by the Canaanites. The veil to cover the face, which at a later date became a necessary part of a woman's costume, had not in those early days come into use. And Isaac brought her into his mother, Sarah's, tent. Isaac had removed three days' journey from Mamre to Beer-lah-roi, and as soon as Rebekah came she was installed in the state tent. After this, Isaac married her, and she appears to have been quite as independent as Sarah.

We do not find that Rebekah's character improved with the passing years as did Sarah's under Divine grace. It should be remembered, however, that while Abraham and Sarah severed themselves from pagan surroundings in a determination to worship the true God, Rebekah and her family, though also worshippers of the true God, had no such incentive.

Rebekah had much to learn, and perhaps much to unlearn, when she came to Isaac; there was, in her, a natural tendency to stray from the path of uprightness and truth which could have been overcome only by Divine grace.

At the end of twenty years twin sons were born to Rebekah and Isaac, and named Esau and Jacob. Rebekah does not appear to have feared the fate of the childless wife as did Sarah by giving her maid to her husband; we learn, however, from *Genesis* 25:21 that it was Isaac himself who believed, as heir to the promises of Abraham, that God would in His own time fulfil His promise of multitudinous seed.

'The character of the younger son, Jacob, was a duplicate of that of his mother. As her pet she trained him, perhaps, unconsciously in her own faults, and clearly he was an apt scholar.

'The sister of Laban, a man full of craft and deceit, was, like her brother, not very open or straightforward. To make a favourite of one of the family, at least so as to show preference is a sign of narrow though perhaps deep affection; but to overreach a husband like Isaac for the injury of one of her two sons was as heartless as it was ignoble. . . . The deceit of Rebekah and Jacob was sorely visited on both. It must have been a great trial to the mother to lose her favourite son forever, for Jacob not only never saw his mother again, but lost all the fruit of his years of toil under his father, and had to begin the world again in Mesopotamia with a very hard master.'[5]

Another aspect of this ancient tale of scheming and duplicity is

---

[5] Cunningham Geikie, D.D., *The Holy Land and the Bible,* pp. 403, 404.

that 'Rebekah thinks—and thousands of people while scanning her story think with her—that she is acting out of a maternal partiality for her younger son. Actually she is merely Jehovah's tool. She takes advantage of an old blind man, but was it not for this moment that he was made blind? . . . Rebekah stands unique as the first woman to challenge the man-instituted rule of primogeniture.

'Thousands of women before her—as after—must have deplored it and grieved over it, seeing in the younger son the more worthy claimant to heirdom; Rebekah is the first woman on record to have made nonsense of it.'[6]

Rebekah's nurse, Deborah, who came with her from Haran upon her marriage to Isaac, appears to have accompanied Jacob when he was sent to his mother's home to escape the wrath of his brother Esau, from whom he had obtained the birthright by deceit.

Had he the patience to wait God's time the birthright would have been his by special gift according to the sure word of promise *(Genesis* 25:23).

Deborah and her brother, Rotheus, were of the family of Abraham—'Chaldeans, God-fearing, free-born and noble.'[7]

Rebekah's death is not recorded in the Scriptures: her son Jacob, however, on his dying couch in Egypt, mentions her burial place as being at Macphelah in the sepulchre with Abraham, Sarah, Isaac and Leah.

[6] N. Lofts, *Women in the Old Testament,* p. 34.
[7] *The Testaments of the Twelve Patriarchs,* trans. by R.H. Charles, D.D., D.Litt.

CHAPTER 3

RACHEL (*Genesis* 29)

The story of Rachel has ever held a fascination for readers of the Scriptures, and this in spite of the fact that our translations, and lack of understanding of ancient terms, have led the reader to believe that Rachel was an idolater and also guilty of theft.

Rachel and Leah are first introduced to us as the daughters of Laban of Haran, who was not himself an idolater, otherwise Jacob would not have been sent to his house by Isaac and Rebekah to obtain a wife.

The courtship of Jacob is one of the most familiar stories of the Bible; the deceit of Laban in giving him Leah instead of his loved Rachel at the end of seven years' service must have brought to Jacob a sharp realization that he was but reaping as he had sown. Jacob served Laban yet another seven years for Rachel and afterwards six years for his cattle.

At the end of twenty years Jacob, after many futile attempts to sever his connection with Laban, decided upon another course: he would steal away from Laban, who was now about to travel to the hills for the annual sheep-shearing, but he must first obtain the consent of his wives, Rachel and Leah, for as the law then stood they could not be compelled to leave their father's house. And so it came to pass that when Jacob called Rachel and Leah to the field to discuss with them this momentous question of leaving Haran, they consented at once saying; 'Is there yet any portion or inheritance for us in our father's house? Are we not counted of him strangers?

for he hath sold us, and hath quite devoured also our money. For all the riches which God hath taken from our father, that is ours, and our children's: now then, whatsoever God hath said unto thee, do.' Thus the die was cast, and Jacob proceeded with his preparations to leave Haran for his father's house at Hebron, taking his two wives and their maids, Zilpah and Bilhah, all the sons and daughters he had by these four mothers, and all his cattle and goods which he had acquired in Haran. Rachel and Leah were well aware that once away from the house at Padan-Aram, their mercenary father, Laban, would sell the property which should be inherited by them and their children; with this knowledge they devised a plan to outwit their father. Rachel, being the stronger character of the two women, was the one to carry it out. With her father, Laban, away from home, Rachel secured the title-deeds to the property which she and Leah should inherit, and hid them in the camel's furniture; this was done unknown to Jacob. Title-deeds and other valuables in those days were known by the general term 'gods;' even today we speak of our 'household gods,' when referring to objects of value which we treasure. Jacob and his household, with all their goods, moved off on their long trek to Hebron. When but three days' journey had been accomplished they were overtaken by Laban pursuing in hot haste after the imposing cavalcade.

Having returned from the hill country, the sheep-shearing over for another year, Laban, finding the Jacob household gone, no doubt derived satisfaction from the thought that now he could do as he wished with his daughters' property, but in this he was completely baulked by the discovery that the title-deeds were gone.

His suspicion at once fell upon Jacob and, pursuing after him, he overtook the party at Mount Gilead. Accusation of Jacob began immediately, which Jacob in astonishment vehemently denied, and invited the irate Syrian to search his stuff and find, if he could, his lost 'gods.' Laban went from tent to tent until he reached Rachel's, and she, calmly apologising for her inability to rise to make the customary curtsey, continued to sit upon the camels' furniture under which she had hidden the precious title deeds.

The crafty Laban, in the belief that, after all, the title-deeds must still be in their place at home, now proceeded to make himself secure against attack from Jacob, in a future day, if his wives should come back to Haran to claim their inheritance, by erecting a heap of stones to be a 'witness.' And Laban said to Jacob, 'This heap be witness and this pillar be witness, that I will not pass over this heap to thee, and that thou shalt not pass over this heap and this pillar unto me, for harm.' Thus was Jacob unconsciously disarmed, and Laban turned his steps homeward to Padan-Aram.

The title-deeds of those ancient times were small tablets of stone or baked clay whereon were inscribed in closely-written characters a description of the property: these documentary evidences of ownership of property were often called 'images,' in the sense of being a representation of such, and were closely guarded, as no claim to ownership could be made without them. Very good examples of these ancient title-deeds may be seen in the British Museum.

We are not left without evidence that Rachel, the wife of Jacob's choice, retained first place in his affections. In the next stage of their journey, when Jacob was obliged to meet Esau and to come in fear and trembling face to face with the brother from whose wrath he had fled twenty years before, it is Rachel and her little son Joseph, now twelve years of age, who are given the place of most protection. 'And he put the handmaids and their children foremost, and Leah and her children after, and Rachel and Joseph hindermost.' The dreaded meeting passed off without any untoward incident, and Jacob came to 'Shalem, a city of Shechem, which is in the land of Canaan.'

While here, God appeared unto Jacob and said, 'Arise, go up to Bethel, and dwell there: and make there an altar unto God, that appeared unto thee when thou fleddest from the face of Esau thy brother.' In preparing to obey this command Jacob gave an order which is often completely misunderstood in the present day: 'Then Jacob said unto his household, and to all that were with him, Put away the strange gods that are among you, and be clean, and change your garments . . . and they gave unto Jacob all the strange gods which were in their hand, and all their earrings which were in their ears; and Jacob hid them under the oak which was by Shechem.' Here again the word translated 'gods' signifies articles of value, and 'strange' is used in the sense of 'new;' possibly jewellery, 'in their hand' denotes rings and bracelets which they had acquired after leaving Haran; the earrings were, in the case of rich people, very valuable. The position was that at Bethel there was a 'makom,' a heathen temple, and marauders lay in wait to rob travellers who came up to the temple to worship; this temple was in course of erection when Jacob passed this way twenty years earlier. The astute Jacob, travelling with his household in considerable state, as all rich men do in the East, wished to go up to Bethel as a poor man so that the cupidity of the inhabitants should not be aroused. And so in obedience to Jacob's command they were 'clean stripped' of their valuables, and changed their beautiful embroidered garments for the garb of poor travellers. Jacob hid all these valuables under an oak at Shechem; according to Josephus the 'gods,' i.e. the title-deeds, were also buried under the oak at Shechem. There is no record of Jacob having collected any of these valuables again, nor is it likely that he did so, for Bethel is many miles south of Shechem, and on the direct route to Hebron, the abode of his father Isaac; they may still await the spade of the archaeologist.

The command of the Almighty to Jacob was, 'Go up to Bethel, and dwell there.' Jacob does not appear to have obeyed this command; eager to reach his father, Isaac's, house, and having visited Bethel as an act of worship, and built there an altar, he appears to have continued his journey south, but camel travelling over long distances was not suited to Rachel's condition and when there was 'but a little way to come to Ephrath,' Rachel's second son, Benjamin, was born.

In commanding Jacob to dwell at Bethel it may have been the Divine will that Rachel should rest there, and that at Bethel her child should be born; if this was so, it must have added greatly to the poignancy of Jacob's grief when Rachel died at Ephrath in giving birth to Benjamin, and Jacob's words on his dying couch: 'Rachel died by me in the land of Canaan . . . when yet there was but a little way to come unto Ephrath,' bear this out.

The pillar or monument which Jacob raised over his beloved Rachel's tomb traditionally remains to the present day—under the superstructure which has been built over it. This monument, known at first as the Hippodrome, was included in her son Benjamin's territory when, under Joshua, the land of Canaan was divided among the twelve tribes.

Rachel's two little sons, Joseph, at this time about twelve years of age, and the infant Benjamin, were at once the solace and anxious care of the grief-stricken Jacob; it is recorded that Bilhah, Rachel's maid, herself nursed the infant Benjamin.

Another great sorrow awaited Jacob when, five years afterwards, Joseph was lost to him through the cruelty of his brothers—to be found some years later as the Prime Minister of Egypt, 'the lord of the country.'

Of Joseph, Jacob in his prophetic blessing declared, 'Joseph is a fruitful bough ... by a well; whose branches run over the wall'—a prophecy which has been amply fulfilled through his two sons: Ephraim, the birthright tribe and leader of Anglo-Saxondom, and in Manasseh, the 'great people' of the United States.

Of his youngest son, Benjamin, Jacob declared: 'Benjamin shall ravin as a wolf: in the morning he shall devour the prey, and at night he shall divide the spoil.' In these words we have a vivid portrayal of the warlike, yet generous, spirit of the descendants of Benjamin.

Joseph inherited his mother, Rachel's, beauty; Benjamin her courageous and adventurous spirit. Benjamin in Egypt became the founder of one of the fiercest tribes in Israel; his fighting proclivities, however, were almost always on the side of justice. It was said of the Benjamites that they were 'sons of terror to their enemies, but sons of succour and strength to their friends.' In this epitome of the character of the younger son of Rachel, the fulfilment of the prophetic blessings of both Jacob and Moses can be plainly discerned.

It is a remarkable fact that the massacre of the children, by the command of Herod, in the hope that the child Jesus would be slain, was carried out in Benjamin's territory, and so was fulfilled the prophecy of Jeremiah,

'Rachel weeping for her children refused to be comforted . . . because they were not.' These words would have been without point had the sufferers been Judah's children, for Leah, not Rachel, was their mother.

The Jews have no legitimate claim on Rachel; it is therefore somewhat absurd to find the Jews making pilgrimage to the tomb of Rachel, as to an ancestress, which they do to the present day.

ZILPAH AND BILHAH

Upon their marriage to Jacob, Leah and Rachel were each given a maid by their father Laban—the maid equivalent to a lady-in-waiting of the present day. In this instance the maids were relatives of the House of Padan-Aram at Haran, for Rotheus their father, with his sister, Deborah, were of the family of Abraham, a 'Chaldean, God-fearing, free-born and noble' and had been taken captive in their youth to be bought back by Laban and adopted into his household. Rotheus married Euno of the House of Padan-Aram. Zilpah and Bilhah were their daughters. Laban, as head of the household, had the disposal of any purchased inmate, and so to Leah he gave Zilpah, and to Rachel, Bilhah.

Bilhah died while mourning for Joseph after he had been reported dead; and was buried near Rachel at Ephratah; she was not, therefore, of the Jacob household which went down to Egypt upon the discovery that Joseph was yet alive. Many years later, upon the death of her sister in Egypt, Joseph commands the sons of Zilpah: 'And carry up Zilpah your mother and lay her near Bilhah by the Hippodrome, near Rachel.'[8]

---

[8] *The Testaments of the Twelve Patriarchs*, trans. by R.H. Charles, D.D., D.Litt.

CHAPTER 4

DINAH (*Genesis* 34)

O f the daughters of Jacob the name of but one has come down to us, and this because of her more exalted position as the daughter of Leah, the chieftainess.

Leah, as the eldest daughter of Laban, took precedence, according to law, in supplying the next chieftainess in line of descent, and Dinah, which signifies the female judge, succeeded Leah as 'tribal mother.' Thus it was that Jacob needed to marry Leah first, and could not have Rachel until Leah's position was thus assured.[9]

According to Josephus, the Jacob household, on its journey south to Hebron, came to Shalem, a city of Shechem, at a time when the inhabitants were keeping a festival, and Dinah went into the city to see the finery of the women. The son of Hamor, the king, the prince of the city, captivated by her beauty and grace, seized her. This treatment of Dinah among these primitive Hivites really meant marriage. 'On her marrying a Hivite her brothers were furious, because she would thus subjugate her judgeship to another race, and only the incorporation of the Hivites with the Israel race by circumcision could remedy the matter.'[10]

The prince and his father begged her in marriage according to Hebrew law and custom, and offered Jacob any price he pleased to obtain her; they even agreed to the carrying out of the rite of circumcision proposed by Dinah's brothers.

Dreading nothing, Shechem and Hamor, by hinting to their

---

[9] Sir Flinders Petrie, *Egypt and Israel.*
[10] Katherine Bushnell, *God's Word to Women,* para. 61.

people how it would gain them the wealth of Jacob and his family, persuaded them to submit to the Hebrew's proposal. On the third day Simeon and Levi, own brothers to Dinah, and perhaps a number of servants, entered the city, slew the inhabitants, and brought away their sister Dinah, who was at the time about fourteen years of age; the other sons of Jacob coming up seized on the spoil. This they did to revenge the treatment of their sister by a non-Hebrew prince.

According to Josephus, 'when Jacob informed his sons of the retention of his daughter in the city of Shechem, the greatest part said nothing, not knowing what advice to give. But Simeon and Levi, the brethren of Dinah by the same mother, agreed between themselves upon the action following. It being now the time of festival when the Shechemites were engaged in feasting and revelry, they fell upon the watch when they were asleep, and coming into the city slew all the males, including the king and his son, but spared the women; and when they had done this without their father's consent they brought away their sister. Now while Jacob was astonished at the greatness of this act, and severely blaming his sons for it, God stood by him and bid him be of good courage; but to purify his tents, and to offer those sacrifices which he had vowed to offer when he went first into Mesopotamia and saw the vision. As he was, therefore, purifying his tents, he happened to light upon the gods (title-deeds) of Laban, for he did not know before that Rachel had secured them, and he hid them in the earth, under an oak at Shechem,'[11] doubtless in the same place and at the same time that he hid the valuables of his household.

From this incident with the Shechemites there emerged two great benefits for Israel: security for their women-folk for it was not until the era of the Judges that non-Hebrews dared to interfere

---

[11] Josephus, *Antiq.*, Bk. I, Chap. XXI.

with them), and the discovery of the title-deeds, enabling Jacob to hide them in a safe place against the day when they will be produced as a witness to the accuracy of the biblical account of the ancient history of Israel.

CHAPTER 5

TAMAR (*Genesis* 38)

Judah, fourth son of Jacob and Leah, in direct disobedience to the Hebrew unwritten law of marrying within their own race—as so signally demonstrated in the cases of Isaac and Jacob in their obtaining wives of their kindred in Haran—married a woman of Canaan.

Three sons were born to them, and as the mother in those ancient times had entire charge of the children, these sons were brought up in the ways of the Canaanites and without that respect for morality which ever marks the worshipper of the true God.

Judah had long since realized his mistake in marrying a woman of Canaan, and determined that his sons should have wives of his own race. A Hebrew lady named Tamar, the daughter of Aram (signifying palm tree), was chosen by Judah for his eldest son, Er. Aram was the son of Abraham's nephew Kemuel (Genesis 22:21).

These sons appear to have been addicted to all the sins and wickednesses of the Canaanites. First, Er died shortly after his marriage, and the next eldest son, Onan, refused to obey the Hebrew Law of the next eldest son by marrying his brother's widow.

Judah became alarmed when Onan died; we are told that the Lord 'slew him also.' Judah now feared to give Tamar to his youngest son, Shelah, 'lest peradventure he die also, as his brethren did.' Judah returned Tamar to her father's house, there to await his pleasure; in the meantime his Canaanite wife, Bathshua, died.

Tamar, in the belief that her father-in-law, Judah, would marry a second time a woman of Canaan, determined to remedy the racial descent problem in her own person. A relative of the Jacob household, and well aware of the necessity for racial purity in that House, Tamar embarked upon a course which would prevent Judah's immediate descendants being other than Hebrew, and a very self-sacrificing course it was.

It was masterly strategy which brought about the meeting of Judah with his widowed daughter-in-law by the wayside, as recorded in the 38th chapter of *Genesis,* and the pledges given by Judah, with which he was later confronted, put all denial beyond peradventure.

Thus, by Tamar's self-sacrificing action, the royal enclosure within the House of Judah was saved from contamination by forbidden blood stock. Tamar was well aware that in taking the course she did to preserve the purity of her race in the House of Judah she ran the risk of being burnt by fire, and it was not until she was brought forth to receive this punishment by her unsuspecting father-in-law's command that she revealed the true state of affairs. 'Discern, I pray thee, whose are these, the signet, the bracelets, and staff.' The signet, or ring, was the emblem of power and authority; the bracelet was the cord, usually of gold, from which the signet was suspended, and the staff, which also signified a sceptre, emblem of authority as head of the tribe.

In the family records which were handed down from father to son, Tamar would learn of the care exercised to preserve purity of race; she would learn that her great ancestor, Noah, 'was a just man and perfect in his generations' from Seth. The word Tamim means whole, flawless.

Twin sons were born to Tamar and named Pharez and Zarah. Pharez became an ancestor of our Lord.

Shelah, the youngest son of Judah and Bathshua, became quite an important House in Israel, but was disqualified, by Divine intervention because of his spurious birth, from becoming an ancestor of the Redeemer of Israel.

Judah, in his 'Story of Tamar,' states that he lived a good and pure life until he met Bathshua, the Canaanite. 'I said to my father-in-law, I will take counsel with my father, and so will I take thy daughter. And he was unwilling, but he shewed me a boundless store of gold in his daughter's behalf; for he was a king. And he adorned her with gold and pearls and caused her to pour out wine for us at the feast. And the wine turned aside my eyes, and pleasure blinded my heart. And I became enamoured of her and I transgressed the commandment of the Lord, and the commandment of my fathers, and I took her to wife. And the Lord rewarded me according to the imagination of my heart, inasmuch as I had no joy in her children. . . . I turned aside to Tamar, and I wrought a great sin. . . . for I gave my staff, that is the stay of my tribe; and my girdle, that is, my power, and, my diadem, that is, the glory of my kingdom.

'And indeed I repented of these things. Wine revealeth the mysteries of God and men, even as I also revealed the commandments of God and the mysteries of Jacob my father to the Canaanitish woman, Bathshua, which God bade me not to reveal. . . . For the sake of money and beauty I was led astray to Bathshua the Canaanite. . . For even wise men among my sons shall they mar, and shall cause the kingdom of Judah to be diminished, which the Lord gave me because of my obedience to my father. For I never caused grief to Jacob my father; for all things whatsoever he commanded I did. And Isaac, the father of my father, blessed me to be king of Israel, and Jacob further blessed me in like manner. And I know that from me shall the kingdom be established.

'For the sake of money I lost my children, and had not my repentance, and my humiliation, and the prayers of my father been accepted I should have died childless. But the God of my fathers had mercy on me because I did it in ignorance.... And I learnt my own weakness while thinking myself invincible.'[12]

Of the four women mentioned in connection with the ancestry of our Lord: Tamar, Rahab, Ruth and Bathsheba, Tamar is the first to have the honour of taking a definite step for racial purity, and it was indeed a great tribute which Judah paid her in his pronouncement, 'She hath been more righteous than I' (*Genesis* 38:26).

---

[12] *The Testaments of the Twelve Patriarchs* (Judah), p. 57, trans. by R.H. Charles, D.D., D.Litt.

CHAPTER 6

MIRIAM (*Exodus* 2; 15; *Numbers* 12)

Three remarkable children were born in Egypt to Amram and Jochebed of the House of Levi. Amram, according to Josephus, was 'one of the nobler sort of the Hebrews.' Miriam, the eldest, was, like her brothers, Moses and Aaron, destined to be an instrument in the hands of Almighty God for the release of Israel from bondage in Egypt.

We first meet Miriam as a young girl, in obedience to her mother, watching from the banks of the river Nile the fate of her baby brother who was by his parents, in faith and hope of preservation, laid in an ark and set among the bulrushes, near the river's edge. It was an exciting moment for Miriam when Princess Thermuthus, Pharaoh's daughter, appeared walking by the river's edge followed by her attendants. The Princess, noticing the ark, sent one of her maids to fetch it. The beauty of the babe appealed irresistibly to the Princess, while his weeping aroused her compassion.

Miriam, watching from the river bank, saw the babe turn away from the Egyptian nurses brought by order of the Princess. Miriam approached as though from curiosity and enquired of the Princess if she might fetch a Hebrew nurse, in case the babe would only be consoled by one of his own race. The Princess agreed at once, and Miriam hurried away to fetch Jochebed, the child's mother. With the now familiar words: 'Take this child away, and nurse it for me, and I will give thee thy wages,' the princess committed the babe, Moses, to the care of his own mother, who bore him home in triumph, accompanied by the no less rejoicing Miriam.

We do not again hear of Miriam until she is a very elderly woman, and as a prophetess and leader of the women, taking part in the exodus from Egypt. After the crossing of the Red Sea Miriam composed a song of deliverance for the women of Israel, of which it would appear that the refrain alone has come down to us. 'And Miriam the prophetess, the sister of Aaron, took a timbrel in her hand; and all the women went out after her with timbrels and with dances. And Miriam answered them, "Sing ye to the Lord, for He hath triumphed gloriously, the horse and his rider hath He thrown into the sea".'

According to Jewish tradition Miriam married Hur of the tribe of Judah; he it was who, with Aaron, 'stayed up his (Moses') hands, the one on the one side, and the other on the other side' until the going down of the sun, when the Amalekites were utterly defeated.

With Aaron, Hur was left in charge of the people while Moses was on Mount Sinai. Bezaleel, the grandson of Miriam and Hur, a clever designer and craftsman, was charged to execute the works of art for the Tabernacle in the wilderness, and was appointed superintendent of the other craftsmen; both he and his assistants executed the work with the utmost exactness.

About one year after the crossing of the Red Sea, Miriam, with Aaron her brother, took umbrage at their brother Moses 'because of the Ethiopian woman he had married.'[13]

The Midianites were descendants of Abraham through Keturah, and were viewed by the descendants of Isaac as inferior in social status, as well as being completely outside the great promises made by Almighty God to the descendants of Isaac. In Egypt Miriam and her brothers enjoyed considerable prestige;

---

[13] The Midianites occupied the territory formerly inhabited by the Ethiopians.

Moses having been brought up at the Court of Pharaoh where he was the acknowledged heir to the throne as the adopted son of Princess Thermuthus, herself next in succession.[14]

Aaron was in Egypt in circumstances superior to those of his people held in bondage, and though their family had no pretensions to sovereign authority by descent, they were of consideration by their property or their office.

Miriam therefore left Egypt as a person of distinction, not only because of her family connections, but as a recognized prophetess, with the additional reputation of possessing the gift of poetry.

Both Miriam and Aaron believed that by his Midianite marriage Moses had forfeited his title to authority over the chosen people, and reproaching him asked if they were not also prophets. 'Hath He not spoken also by us?' They quarrelled with Moses as though he now managed affairs by the advice of his Midianite wife (who had succeeded Zipporah), and had not consulted them in the affairs of the elders. Although Miriam did have a Divine mission, it was necessary that she and Aaron should learn once and for all that Moses was the Divinely-appointed leader vested with authority to bring the children of Israel through the wilderness to the Promised Land. 'And the Lord spake suddenly unto Moses, and unto Aaron, and unto Miriam, Come out ye three unto the tabernacle of the congregation. And they three came out. And the Lord came down in the pillar of the cloud, and stood in the door of the tabernacle, and called Aaron and Miriam; and they both came forth. And He said, Hear now My words: if there be a prophet among you, I the Lord will make Myself known unto him in a vision. . . . My servant Moses is not so, who is faithful in all Mine house. With him will I speak mouth to mouth, even apparently, and not in dark speeches; and the similitude of the Lord will he behold: wherefore then were

---

[14] Josephus, *Antiq.*, Bk. II, Chap. IX.

ye not afraid to speak against My servant Moses? And the anger of the Lord was kindled against them; and He departed. And the cloud departed from off the tabernacle and, behold, Miriam became leprous, as white as snow; and Aaron looked upon Miriam, and, behold, she was leprous. And Aaron said unto Moses, Alas, my lord, I beseech thee, lay not the sin upon us, wherein we have done foolishly, and wherein we have sinned. Let her not be as one dead. . . . And Moses cried unto the Lord, saying, Heal her now, O God, I beseech Thee. And the Lord said unto Moses . . . Let her be shut out from the camp seven days, and after that let her be received in again. . . . And the people journeyed not till Miriam was brought in again.'

In this signal manner was the authority of Moses established, never again to be questioned; he was the Divinely-appointed supreme leader, and recognized as such until the end of his days.

It is certain that the Hebrews brought leprosy with them from Egypt, for at the very commencement of their forty years' wanderings Moses commanded that every leper should be put out of the camp, and the disease could not have been brought on in the wilderness.

In this connection Moses commanded the Israelites to abstain from pork, leprosy being a disease to which the pig is liable. In studying the Bible account of leprosy it should be borne in mind that the Mosaic Law had in view a wide class of diseases, the symptoms of which were eruptions on the skin.

Thus the words which we translate 'leper,' 'leprous,' and 'leprosy' were undoubtedly used in a loose and general way and not in every instance is true leprosy intended.

Miriam's mission as a leader in Israel came to an end almost at the completion of the forty years in the wilderness; her death took place in the same year as that of Aaron; she was buried at Kadesh, not far from Mount Hor, the burial-place of Aaron.

The prophet, Micah, in a review of the way in which the children of Israel had been led and guided, declares, 'For I brought thee up out of the land of Egypt, and redeemed thee out of the house of servants; and I sent before thee Moses, Aaron and Miriam' (6:4).

Miriam's name is thus recorded as not only an illustrious woman of Israel, but as a leader who had a great part to play in the exodus from Egypt and wilderness training, as organizer and superintendent of the women's welfare; her task was an onerous one, calling for ability in leadership, and resourcefulness in a new and untried path.

CHAPTER 7

RAHAB (*Joshua* 2)

The story of Rahab begins, actually, at the time Joseph brought his two sons, Manasseh and Ephraim, to his aged father's couch to receive the patriarchal blessing. Jacob (Israel) recited the great covenant blessings of multiplicity of seed and accession of land to be inherited by his descendants, in fulfilment of the Abrahamic Covenant.

In addition Jacob now bestowed on Joseph's younger son, Ephraim, the birthright, with which went leadership and all the privileges of the firstborn.

These were strange words to fall upon the ears of the young boy, Ephraim: 'His younger brother (Ephraim) shall be greater than he (Manasseh) . . . and he set Ephraim before Manasseh,'

Ephraim was already a very important boy; his mother was the Princess of On, of the Royal House of Egypt; his father, Joseph, Prime Minister of Egypt, 'the lord of the country,' who had proved himself a man of exceptional ability and wisdom. The tribe of Ephraim was ennobled at its source by descent from the Princess of On—as all Israel was ennobled by descent from Sarah who was titled Queen of the multitude that their seed was to become.

Ephraim, brought up at the exclusive Court of Egypt, received the best education the world could afford, Egypt at that time being the centre of the world's culture.

Ephraim, grown to manhood, married and had three sons, the names of whom are recorded in *Numbers* 26:35. They were brought up in the knowledge of the inherited blessings bestowed not only on the Israel family but those special promises of which the descendants of Ephraim were to be heirs. These family traditions were passed on to Ephraim's grandsons, whose names are recorded in I *Chronicles* 7:20, 21. These three sons and six grandsons of Ephraim became impatient to enter upon their inheritance. The latter were the sixth in descent from Abraham, with whom the great land covenant was made (*Genesis* 15:18).

Here were the descendants of Abraham in Egypt, and in Egypt they seemed likely to remain. These sons of Ephraim decided to visit the land of Canaan and perhaps make a beginning in the colonization of the land.

There was no difficulty in obtaining a footing in the Promised Land, for at that time and for long afterwards Canaan was under the overlordship of Egypt.

The sons of Ephraim would, therefore, enter Canaan with a good measure of prestige as princes of Israel living in close contact with the Egyptian Court. All might have gone well, the Canaanites tolerating if not welcoming their settlement in the land, but for the behaviour of the would-be colonizers 'whom the men of Gath . . . slew, because they came down to take away their cattle' (I *Chronicles* 7:21).

The reason for this act of robbery is difficult to understand. It was certainly not induced by lack of funds. Over-confidence in the success of the expedition may possibly have led them to take the cattle for the purpose of a sacrificial thank-offering. This premature attempt to enter upon their inheritance, and its tragic sequel are recorded in I *Chronicles* 7:20, 22: 'And Ephraim their father mourned many days, and his brethren came to comfort him.' All these princes of Israel, Ephraim's heirs, were slain by the men of Gath. What a tragedy! Where now the birthright? Where now the succession to the inheritance? But in his old age Ephraim had another son who was given the dismal name of Beriah, 'because it went evil with his house.'

Beriah grew to manhood and married; the ninth in descent from this youngest son was Joshua, the one appointed to lead Israel into the Promised Land.

Moses, of the tribe of Levi, shepherded the Israelites out of Egypt and through the wilderness, there to give them by God's command the laws and ordinances which would guide them in their national and spiritual life. But only one of the birthright tribe, Ephraim, could conduct them over the river Jordan.

Moses brought them almost to the brink of this river, and from the highest peak on Mount Nebo, Pisgah, in their first inheritance, 'the land of Moab,' on the east side of the river, he was permitted to view the Promised Land. Here his splendid and faithful leadership came to an end. There is another important link in the chain of events between the time of Ephraim and that of Joshua. Sherah, the daughter of Beriah, went into the land of Canaan and settled there. This great chieftainess proceeded to build three cities or castles, Beth-horon the Lower, Beth-horon the Upper, and Uzzen-sherah, or the Stronghold of Sherah (I *Chronicles* 7:24). That Sherah was already married, and had a family, also many servants and attendants, is evident from the fact that so much building was necessary in order to accommodate this important woman and her retinue.

Here, in the centre of Canaan, Sherah, the great granddaughter of the Princess of On and Joseph, took up her abode, and here her descendants lived until they were joined by their kinsmen of Israel, under their great leader, Joshua, also of the birthright tribe of Ephraim.

We can imagine the stories that would be passed on from one generation to another in Sherah's family; of their past glories in

Egypt; of their royal descent; their birthright as Ephraimites, and they would hear from time to time of the reverse of fortune suffered by their kinsmen in Egypt when 'there arose up a new king over Egypt, which knew not Joseph;' of the bondage; the exodus; the wilderness training; the first conquest under Moses of 'the land of Moab' on the east side of the river Jordan.

With all these events in Israel's national life these families descended from Sherah would be more or less acquainted, and when to one of these families Rahab was born, she was given this name which signifies 'remembering Egypt,' in token of her people's pride in their connection with Egypt in days now long past. No Canaanite would dream of giving a child such a name 'remembering Egypt;' they would have no occasion to do so. The Egyptians were their overlords to whom the Canaanites paid tribute.

With the aid of archaeology we can now obtain a clear picture of Canaan in the time of Joshua. The Tel-el-Amarna tablets, discovered in 1887 among the ruins of the palace of the Egyptian King Amenhotep IV, consist very largely of letters from native Canaanite rulers to their overlords, and are full of appeal for help against the Israelite invaders.[15] The tablets show that in each of the Canaanite cities of Palestine, there was, in addition to the native ruler or king, an Egyptian official called, according to Major Conder, a Paka, who was, presumably, placed there to guard the Egyptian interests.

For no reason which appears the Egyptians withdrew their troops from Canaan. Major Conder remarks: 'The Egyptian troops had been withdrawn from Palestine in the year that the Israelites came out of the desert.'[16] This explains the words of Joshua, in his report to Moses, as one of the twelve spies sent out to view the land

[15] Sir Charles Marston, *The Bible Comes Alive,* pp. 89-108.
[16] Palestine Fund Reports, Conder's Handbook.

of Canaan: 'their defence is departed from them.'

The house of the Paka, equivalent to our modern Embassy, would naturally be in a prominent position, such as the town wall, and close to the Citadel. The Tel-el-Amarna tablets give the name of one Egyptian representative in Canaan: Zimrida, Governor of Lachish.[17]

Archaeology may yet reveal the name of the Egyptian Paka in Jericho in the days of Joshua.

We shall now return to Rahab, and try to ascertain how the obnoxious appellation, 'harlot,' came to be attached to her. In Eastern languages the same word is often used for 'harlot' and 'widow' as, for instance, in the Urdu language. The same word would appear to describe a woman no longer a virgin, but without a husband, whether she had been legally married or not. It is a striking fact that in the Authorized Version of the Scriptures, Jeroboam's mother, Zeruah, is recorded as 'a widow woman' (I *Kings* 11:26) while in the Septuagint the word used is 'harlot.'

If the translators had inserted 'widow' in the margin opposite Rahab's name in *Joshua,* chapter 2, it would at once have been clear to the reader that 'harlot' and widow' were interchangeable terms.

Ferrar Fenton, in his translation, omits the moral status of Zeruah, while Rahab is put down as an 'innkeeper,' and by Coverdale as a 'taverner.' These are but brave attempts to clear the fair name of Rahab from the objectionable term 'harlot.' 'Innkeeper' and 'taverner,' however, convey no historical truth, for in the East the inns or khans had neither host nor hostess.

The Septuagint, from which our Authorized Version is derived, was translated at a time when the women of Israel had lost almost all their social status, through contact with the Babylonians

---

[17] *The Bible Comes Alive*, p. 112.

during the captivity. The Rabbis, therefore, would be at no pains to convey the truth regarding the moral or social standing of any woman.[18]

As for Rahab's presence in Jericho and not with her Israel kinsfolk in one of the Beth-horon cities, the situation now seems to explain itself. The Egyptian representatives had departed upon the withdrawal of the troops from Canaan. It would appear that the last Paka in Jericho had died and his widow, Rahab, did not vacate the Embassy. Though not encouraged, it was not forbidden to Israelites to intermarry with Egyptians; therefore, Rahab, in marrying the Paka, was guilty of no breach of Israel law, nor of disobedience to a Divine Command.

The house, which has been identified as that of Rahab's, astride the walls of Jericho, is in the position the Paka's would have been. 'At the north-west end of the city stood the great Citadel or Migdol whose walls still rise to nearly forty feet. Rahab's house was astride the walls not far from this building... Rahab's house did not share the destruction of the falling of the walls, since she and her family were saved alive. The proximity of the Citadel certainly appears to have held up the walls in the neighbourhood in its immediate vicinity. It is evident, therefore, that Rahab's house adjoined the Citadel.'[19] This is precisely where we should expect to find the Egyptian Embassy, a specially-appointed official building as the 'House on the Wall' where Rahab lived.

We shall now go over to the other side of the river Jordan

---

[18] In Cruden's *Concordance*, under the word 'harlot' we read: 'Some think that she was only an hostess or inn-keeper; and that this is the true signification of the original word. Had she been a woman of ill-fame, say they, would Salmon, a prince of the house of Judah, and one of our Saviour's ancestors, have taken her to wife, or could he have done it by the law? Besides, the spies of Joshua would hardly have gone to lodge with a prostitute, a common harlot: they who were charged with so nice and dangerous a commission.'

[19] *The Bible Comes Alive*, p. 84.

where Joshua is making careful preparation for the conquest of Canaan. Joshua is determined to take no step but at Jehovah's command; he will not make the mistake of his forefathers in their premature attempt to anticipate their inheritance. The Israelites are instructed in the part each one must play in the conquest, and they are brought into perfect obedience to their leader, Joshua, who himself takes his instructions from the great Leader and Commander, the 'Captain of the hosts of the Lord.' Joshua's first step is to send two spies, to 'view the land, even Jericho. And they went, and came into an harlot's (widow's) house, named Rahab.'

It is evident from these words that Joshua was well aware of his kinswoman's presence in Jericho, and sent the two spies to her house. This is borne out in the reference to the spies by St. James where they are termed 'messengers.' Messengers are sent on a specific errand to a definite place or address. Arrived there, they were welcomed by the Lady Rahab, and once over her threshold they were safe, for the Embassy was extra-territorial and so the spies, or messengers, had the privilege of being outside Canaanitish territory.

The news of their arrival soon reached the native ruler, or king of Jericho; he sent his officials to Rahab with the request, 'Bring forth the men that are come to thee, which are entered into thine house.'

But why this request? Why not send his officials into Rahab's house to institute a search? Because no native could enter the Embassy uninvited. The spies were now legally in Egypt. In this incident may be seen the strong line of demarcation between Rahab and the Canaanites among whom she lived.

Although the Egyptian representative was no longer at the Embassy the Canaanites did not admit that the Egyptians had withdrawn permanently, for one letter from the King of Jerusalem to Amenhotep complains: 'Since the Egyptian troops have gone away quitting the land of the King my lord ... let him be kind, and let him regard the entreaties' etc.[20]

Rahab, in conversation with the spies says, 'I know that Jehovah hath given you the land.' Not only in her use of the memorial name, Jehovah, but in her knowledge of the great Land Covenant does Rahab prove herself to be an Israelite, though her ancestors for eight or nine generations had been separated from the main body of Israel. It is this fact which makes Rahab anxious to be assured that when the conquest does take place, she and her kindred will be secured against the fate of the iniquitous and idolatrous Canaanites.

The 'line of scarlet thread' was to mark off the Embassy for the invading Israelites, and so once again the redemption colour was the token of safety for Israelites 'in Egypt.' When the spies returned to the camp, they brought from Rahab precisely the news which Joshua wished to learn: 'All the inhabitants of the land faint because of you.'

The conquest, therefore, would not be difficult. Who but one of his kinsfolk could or would supply this information for use of the Israelite leader?

While Joshua on the east side of Jordan made preparation to cross the river—the vanguard being composed of warriors from the tribes of Reuben, Gad and the half tribe Manasseh, according to their promise given to Moses (*Joshua* 22:1-4)—Rahab was occupied in sending urgent messages to her family and kindred in Beth-horon the Upper and Lower, and Uzzen-Sherah, to come to her in the Egyptian Embassy for safety. No time must be lost, for presently 'Jericho was straitly shut up because of the children of Israel: none went out and none came in.' And when in due course

---

[20] Conder, p. 142.

the walls of Jericho fell, and its utter destruction compassed, Joshua sent the same two young spies to the intact Egyptian Embassy to bring out 'Rahab, and her father, and her mother, and her brethren and all that she had; and they brought out all her kindred (many families), and left them without the camp of Israel.' The families of Israel in the cities of Sherah would, by the eighth generation, have increased to a considerable number of persons; they were, however, all housed in safety within the walls of the Embassy.

How helpful they would be to Joshua in the conquest of Canaan. They prepared the way for the settlement of their brethren in the Land of Promise, as Joseph prepared the way for the settlement of his brethren in Egypt.

These Israelites, with Rahab taking a leading part, were the Divinely-chosen pioneers in the entering in of the Israel people to their inheritance.

These Israel families, housed in the Egyptian Embassy for safety, were, we have sought to show, Ephraimites, and as such were entitled to the privileges of the first-born or leading tribe. 'For with a strong hand hath the Lord brought thee out of Egypt' (*Exodus* 13:9). 'When Israel was a child, then I loved him, and called my son out of Egypt' (*Hosea* 11:1).

When the infant Jesus was taken into Egypt for safety, He was brought out in fulfilment of the prophecy, 'Out of Egypt have I called My son' (*Matthew* 2:15). This is the last and final occasion upon which Egypt is referred to in Scripture as a place of refuge for an Israelite.

That the rulers of Egypt gave help to Israel in their conquest of Canaan may be gathered from both the Scriptures and the Tel-el-Amarna tablets. The 'hornet' was the badge of Thotmes III and his successors. Joshua, at God's command, reminds Israel, 'I sent the hornet before you, which drove them out from before you, even the two kings of the Amorites; but not with thy sword, or with thy bow.'

Sir Charles Marston, from archaeological research, agrees that Israel did have such help from the rulers of Egypt east of Jordan, and also in the withdrawal from Palestine of all Egyptian troops, when Israel came out of the wilderness.

The reason for the friendly attitude of Egypt towards Israel at this time may be found in the fact that Queen Thyi, the wife of Amenhotep II, and mother of Amen-hotep IV, came from Northern Syria which was inhabited by descendants of Terah.

This fair, blue-eyed queen of the Egyptian monuments could, therefore, claim kinship with the descendants of Terah's son, Abraham, who, it will be remembered, was declared by the children of Heth to be 'a mighty prince among us' (*Genesis* 23:6). Rahab, the widow, married Prince Salma, or Salmon, of the House of Pharez-Judah, and so was brought into the exclusive and royal family from which the House of David was built (*Matthew* 1:5).

No woman of questionable character would have been admitted to this Divinely-protected royal enclosure, for marriage with a Canaanite was strictly forbidden *(Deuteronomy* 7:1-3).

Rahab's son, Boaz, married Ruth. Consequently Ruth's mother-in-law by her first marriage, Naomi, and that by her second marriage, Rahab, were women destined to be famous in history, and to have their names recorded in the lineage of Israel's Redeemer and King.

It is a striking fact that the *Epistle to the Hebrews* and the *Epistle of James* (addressed to the 'twelve tribes scattered abroad'), are both addressed primarily to Israelites, and that mention is made of the strength of faith and character of their ancestors, Rahab of Jericho being one of them. 'By faith . . . Rahab perished not with them that believed not, when she had received the spies with peace' *(Hebrews* 11:31). The Greek word used here for peace— eirene—connotes unity; unity, surely, in identity of race with the messengers sent by Joshua.

'Was not Rahab . . . justified by works, when she had received the messengers, and had sent them out another way?' *(James* 2:25). Justify—dikaios—I defend the cause of—I acquit and justify. Rahab defended the cause of her people Israel in the help she was able to render Joshua in his conquest plans.

Rahab's faith was the faith of an Israelite; the faith of one who, like Abraham, was justified by works, and likewise, with faithful Abraham, received the commendation and blessing of the God of Israel.

CHAPTER 8

RUTH (Book of *Ruth)*

Τhe story of Ruth provides a beautiful illustration, of the Redemption Law of Israel, while its pastoral theme is an abiding delight. In these pages, however, the story is presented in the light of the origin of Ruth and Orpah, with special emphasis on Ruth's place in the royal line of the House of David and as an ancestress of our Lord.

Of prime importance in this study is the understanding where, precisely, lay the territory known as 'the land of Moab' which enters so largely into the story of Ruth.

The route taken by the Israelites upon leaving Egypt is traced along the borders of Edom and Moab until they reached the river Arnon: immediately upon crossing the Arnon and in prospect of a speedy entrance into the Promised Land, having arrived at Beerelim 'the well of heroes,' they broke forth into 'the song of the well' *(Numbers* 21:17). The Israelites now had a formidable foe to meet in Sihon, king of the Amorites, whose territory extended from the river Arnon along the northern shores of the Dead Sea and the east side of the river Jordan to the river Jabbok. This territory had been wrested from Moab by the Amorite king and now came into the hands of the Israelites by conquest.

The next conquest of the Israelites was over Og, king of Bashan, who ruled in the territories east of the Sea of Galilee and the north-eastern portion of the valley of the Jordan.

The Israelites were now in possession of all the territory from the river Arnon in the south to Mount Hermon in the north. The river Arnon was thus the dividing line between the territory of racial Moab and that of Israel. Of the territory of Moab and Edom south of the Arnon the Almighty had declared through Moses, 'I will not give thee of their land for a possession.'

Under the leadership of Moses the Israelites acquired all the territory east of Jordan which gave them free access to the river Jordan, and completed their conquest of all the territory from the Arnon to Mount Hermon.

This country east of the river Jordan, a land of unparalleled fertility, appealed irresistibly to the tribes of Reuben, Gad and Manasseh as being extremely desirable for their great herds of cattle. It was a combination of rich arable and pasture land with fine forests. Here the tribes of Reuben, Gad and the half tribe of Manasseh desired to have their allotment. Moses granted their request upon certain conditions, with which they faithfully complied *(Numbers* 32:1-40). These two and a half tribes settled down on an inheritance which brought them great wealth and prosperity. Numerically they increased so rapidly that they were able to send 120,000 men fully armed to King David's coronation at Hebron.

The territory continued under its ancient name, 'land of Moab,' during its Amorite occupation, and when now by conquest it became the possession of the Israelites the name was not altered by the new owners.

Moses leaves posterity in no doubt as to the location of the newly-acquired 'land of Moab' as distinct from the Moabite territory south and south-east of the Dead Sea to which racial Moab was now confined. On nine occasions the great leader describes the new Israelite possession as 'the land of Moab by Jordan opposite Jericho.' There is no ambiguity here. It cannot be made to mean the territory occupied by racial Moab.

It is perfectly clear from *Deuteronomy* 2:34 that every man, woman and child was driven out of the 'land of Moab' in obedience to the Divine command 'for the wickedness of these nations the Lord doth drive them out from before thee.'

Immediately after this cleansing the two and a half tribes took possession, and so it became and continued purely Israelite territory, as Jephthah, after 300 years of Israel ownership, in his argument with the Ammonites, informs them.

From this 'land of Moab' Moses was permitted to view the Promised Land of Canaan and on its highest peak (Pisgah) he died. It cannot be maintained that Moses delivered the Law or any part of it to Israel in the country of racial Moab when they had recently acquired the Moabite territories of Sihon and Og, nor that it was in the land of racial Moab that this great leader died, for Mount Nebo was situated in their new territory, 'by Jordan opposite Jericho.'

Gilead, in the land of Moab, is mentioned as the home of Jair, of Jephthah and of Elijah, who returned here at the end of his long life to be taken up 'into heaven.' It was the refuge of Israelites from the Philistines, of Saul's sons, of David when fleeing from Absalom who followed him thither. The crossing and recrossing of Jordan by David and his household are recorded in the second Book of *Samuel,* chapter 19.

The country on the west side of Jordan conquered and inhabited by the remaining tribes of Israel, that is the nine and a half tribes who passed over the river Jordan under Joshua's leadership, continued to be known by its ancient title, 'land of Canaan,' and, dissociated from its pre-conquest heathen ownership, entered quite largely into Christian expression and hymnology.

The casual reader could easily imagine that the personnel of David's bodyguard were non-Israelites. One of the Apostles,

Simon, though actually an Israelite, was called a Canaanite through being a native of Cana in Galilee. His appellation, 'The Zealot,' comes from the Hebrew, 'canna,' zealous; in Greek, Zelotes. It is, therefore, not remarkable that the territory on the east side of Jordan should continue to be known by its original title, 'land of Moab,' and its inhabitants referred to as Moabites.

The racial Moabites were the determined enemies of the Israelites and much fighting was called for to keep them within their own boundaries. David subdued them at one time, as recorded in I *Chronicles* 18:2. At a later date Jehoshaphat won a great battle over the Moabites. *Jeremiah,* chapter 48, is wholly devoted to the 'land of Moab' on the east side of Jordan occupied by the Israelites. Of the numerous references to Moab in the Old Testament more than one half concern Moab on the east side of Jordan in the occupation of Israel.

After the death of Joshua, whose energetic leadership brought Israel into possession of their inheritance, the Promised Land, and in the beginning of the time of the Judges, a famine occurred in the recently-acquired land of Canaan. As recorded in the Book of *Ruth,* a family of Bethlehem-Judah, Elimelech, Naomi, and their two delicate boys, Mahlon and Chilion, crossed the river Jordan to the 'land of Moab' which was, at the time, in sharp contrast to the land of Canaan, a place of peace and plenty.

Elimelech, a member of the princely House of Pharez-Judah, with his little family sought and found refuge from stress of circumstances and want among their own kith and kin, and they are not alone in the Scripture records as having had intercourse with their brethren on the east side of Jordan. It is not logical, apart from other evidence, to suppose that this family of Israelites should cross the Jordan to their own 'land' or 'country' of Moab, occupied by their fellow Israelites, which was well watered and where there were no famine conditions, and pass through it to reach the Arnon, then cross this considerable river to reach enemy country as was the land of racial Moab. Food was their object and the eastern tribes possessed it in abundance. Here, therefore, they found all things needful for their sustenance, and here they settled down to await the coming of relief to the homeland in Judea.

The sojourn in 'the land of Moab' proved to be a time of sorrow for Naomi in the loss of her husband, Elimelech, and later her two sons, Mahlon and Chilion. 'And they took them wives of the women of Moab; the name of the one was Orpah, and the name of the other Ruth.' There is no indication in the Scripture records to which of the eastern Israelite tribes these young women belonged. In view of the fact that 'Ruth' and 'Reuben' have very largely the same meaning, namely, 'friendship,' it is more than probable that it was to this tribe that Ruth belonged.

It was not permitted to Israelites to marry women of racial Moab; such unions would have met with immediate and condign punishment *(Numbers* 25:1-8). In further support of Ruth's Israel origin is the fact that her reputed historian, the prophet Samuel, could not consistently enforce the Divine command, 'A Moabite shall not enter into the congregation of the Lord; even to their tenth generation shall they not enter into the congregation of the Lord for ever' *(Deuteronomy* 23:3), and at the same time condone so flagrant a disregard of that command on the part of a prince of Pharez-Judah, as was Ruth's first husband, Mahlon, and also her second husband, Boaz. This racial Law never was cancelled nor annulled. The House of Ephratah and all those connected with it were fully aware of the sacred charge which had been given into their hands not only for those days but for future generations. The people of Bethlehem-Ephratah seem always to have been a people apart as though conscious of a determined destiny in the Divine plan for the Israel nation. Even in their dress they differed from the main body of Israel; thus the dress of Naomi, this lady of the exclusive House of Ephratah in Bethlehem, differed considerably in design and detail from the remainder of Western Israel and markedly so from the dress of the people of Eastern Israel, or trans-Jordania from whence came Ruth and Orpah, Naomi's daughters-in-law.

At the end of a residence of ten years in 'the land of Moab,' on the opposite side of Jordan, Naomi decided to return to her home in Bethlehem-Judah, having heard that the famine conditions were past and that 'the Lord had visited His people in giving them bread.' Her daughters-in-law prepare to accompany her, for as Israelites they are acquainted with the Mosaic law which enjoins that 'the wife of the dead shall not marry without unto a stranger.' When, however, Naomi and her retinue, accompanied by Ruth and Orpah, began the journey to Bethlehem it is evident that Naomi believed that her daughters-in-law were but accompanying her part of the way, perhaps to the banks of the river Jordan, as revealed by the conversation which followed the halt called by Naomi. Also she was aware that no thought other than the strict observance of the Mosaic law had entered the minds of these young widows, Ruth and Orpah, hence her argument, 'If I should have an husband . . . and should also bear sons; would ye tarry for them till they were grown?' And so Naomi proceeds to release them from the legal tie which bound them to her as widows of her departed sons.

According to the marriage law, at that time in force, a woman remained with her own people after marriage, and also in the event of widowhood and re-marriage to her late husband's nearest kinsman. This marriage law, which was observed by Israel and non-Israel nations alike, could under exceptional circumstances be set aside, of which there are several instances in the Scripture records.

Naomi's advice to these young widows to return to their people, is evidence that they had never left the maternal roof, and also that Naomi had been living in close proximity to them, for she says, 'The Lord deal kindly with you, as ye have dealt with the dead, and with me.'

Orpah, not difficult to persuade, returns to her people. Ruth heeds not the words of release and advice to return, but pours out her heart to Naomi in the immortal words, 'Intreat me not to leave thee, or to return from following after thee: for whither thou goest, I will go; and where thou lodgest, I will lodge: thy people shall be my people, and thy God my God: where thou diest, will I die, and there will I be buried: Jehovah do so to me, and more also' (literally, 'May Jehovah slay me and worse'), 'if ought but death part thee and me.' All words in italics in the Scriptures are supplied by the translators and are not in the translations they copied from: 'Thy people *(shall be)* my people—Thy God my God.' In the actual words spoken Ruth points out to Naomi that leaving her own family is not so great a sacrifice in view of the fact that they are one in race and worship.

We read in *Ruth* 1:15 that Naomi refers to Orpah as having 'gone back unto her people, and unto her gods.' The Hebrew word used by Naomi is Elohim, which carries several meanings, amongst them God, angels, goddess, gods, judges, etc. Therefore, this word might, as correctly, have been translated 'judges,' and the context warrants this translation. The same word, 'gods,' occurs in *Exodus* 22:28 and against it in the marginal note the word 'judges' is written. Elohim-judges were those representing God in His nation Israel, dispensing justice for God in judging His people. The judges would, Naomi assured her daughters-in-law, see to it that they were provided with husbands from among their own people in view of the fact that their late husbands left no brothers to carry on the name. Naomi, true worshipper of Jehovah, would have had no use for heathen gods or their devotees; she would grieve, indeed, at any indication of defection or backsliding on the part of the trans-Jordanic tribes. The use of the title 'Jehovah' is evidence that Ruth was of pure Israel stock; that Holy name 'Jehovah' was to be a memorial between the Ever-Living and His chosen nation unto all generations. Ruth's words were prompted by a deep religious feeling.

Naomi had reasons for returning to Bethlehem-Judah other than those of freedom from want and the call of home. The seventh jubilee was near when 'the parcel of land' reverted back to Naomi as the widow of Elimelech, but both her sons having died also, there was no male person to take it as the inheritance of the family. By Boaz marrying Ruth this difficulty was overcome. The Jubilee was the crowning enforcement of Israel's Sabbath system. Not only every seventh day but every seventh year, and not only every seventh year but after every seven times seven years there was to be a Sabbath. The Jubilee was a Sabbath year. It had a religious object as well as a humanizing one.

Of the journey from 'the land of Moab' to Bethlehem-Judah taken by Naomi and Ruth no details are recorded, but the story of their arrival at the beginning of barley harvest (in the month of April) is recorded in a beautiful word picture *(Ruth* 1:19-22). How glad Naomi would be of the companionship of the lovely young matron, Ruth, whose unselfish devotion was to cheer and gladden her sorrowing heart and to solace her declining years.

Naomi had evidently sent messengers beforehand to have her home made ready. When they arrived at the gate of Bethlehem they were given a civic welcome and 'all the city was stirred by their arrival' (Moffatt). A city is not usually moved over a couple of travel-stained, weary women arriving at its gates, one of them returning after an absence often years. Rather as the widows of princes of the great House of Pharez-Judah they arrived in all the eastern pomp and state which befitted their rank. The title of 'prince' for the Chiefs of Houses is well established in the Scriptures. How glad the people were to have Naomi again amongst them; she had been in all probability 'the lady bountiful' and greatly missed. The people can scarcely believe that she has come back again, they say questioningly, 'Is this Naomi?' The sound of her name strikes a sad note. From her sorrowing heart come the words of grief and disappointment. 'Call me not Naomi (pleasant), call me Mara (bitter): for the Almighty hath dealt very bitterly with me. I went out full, and the Lord hath brought me home again empty: why call ye me Naomi, seeing the Lord hath testified against me, and the Almighty hath afflicted me?' Not yet, so blinded is she by painful memories and the sense of loss, can Naomi see the purpose of Almighty God in bringing her home again 'empty.' Nor can she have any idea of the great part she has yet to play in the building of the House of David as the guide and guardian of Ruth, her son's widow, until she is wedded to Prince Boaz of the same kindred as her departed husband.

The name Mara, assumed by Naomi instead of her former one, is one which, in the form of Mary, became a notable one in Israel and in this same place, Bethlehem. 'So Naomi returned, and Ruth the Moabitess, her daughter-in-law, with her.' Ruth, belonging as she did to a country still known as the 'land of Moab,' it was natural and quite in accord with usage in those ancient times that Ruth should be called a Moabitess or 'a lady of Moab.' There are numerous instances of this in Scripture.

It is significant that immediately upon settling down in Bethlehem, Ruth, with Naomi's consent, went out to glean in the fields. The 'city' of Bethlehem stands on an eminence 2,500 feet above the sea, its slopes terraced into hanging gardens and a pleasant valley lying underneath on its three sides, while the eastern end is almost touched by the wilderness of Judea. From this fertile grain-producing valley, Bethlehem, 'House of Bread,' derives, linked as it often was to the more ancient name of Ephratah. It is significant that here was born He Who is the 'Bread of Life.' As they looked down on the harvest fields in the valley Naomi and Ruth could observe the harvest operations in progress. In those days assisting in this work was an honourable occupation for women in any station of life so Ruth only wanted to do what many others were happily engaged in.

Having chosen the field in which she wished to work Ruth, later in the day, met the owner of the estate, Boaz, her late husband's kinsman 'who was of the kindred of Elimelech.' There was no difficulty in recognizing this important personage as he strode into the field wearing his scarlet cloak, the insignia of his rank as chief.[21] As the star guided the Magi to Bethlehem so the unseen hand of God directed Ruth to the fields of Boaz.

Ruth in conversation with Boaz refers to herself as a 'stranger.' The word used by Ruth is 'Nokri' and not 'zar' which is the word used only for an alien and of another race, but Ruth is speaking of herself as one strange to those of her own blood and in the land which she had not visited hitherto. The word 'Nokri' in the Hebrew is, therefore, the correct term for the sort of stranger Ruth was. An Australian, though of the British race, would refer to himself as a 'stranger' in this country. 'The land beyond the Jordan' from which Ruth came was, by virtue of its position, as a portion and yet not a portion of Israel, invested with a touching interest in that it was to the main body of Israel emphatically the

---

[21] J.L. Porter, D.D., *The Giant Cities of Bashan*, p. 193.

land of exiles—the refuge of exiles. [22] In addition, the trans-Jordanic tribes, beginning with Reuben, inclined to separation when they began to fall into idolatry, and gradually lost all community of interest with the western tribes.

'Under whose wings thou art come to trust' *(Ruth* 2:12). These words have been taken to mean that Ruth was hitherto an idolater and on coming to Bethlehem had changed over to the worship of Jehovah. This assumption is based upon a misunderstanding of Hebrew terms. David begs of the Almighty to hide him under His wings; to protect and defend him as a hen doth her chickens under her wings *(Psalm* 17:8). Ruth was brought up under matriarchal law then still in force; it was thus a most unusual proceeding for a woman to leave her own people to reside at her husband's home; yet Ruth courageously broke through custom and, trusting in the protection of Jehovah, came to another part of Israel, a part entirely unknown to her, in the belief that there the Lord would make provision for her. There is also the possibility that if the tribe from which Ruth came, probably either Gad or Reuben, or a Levitical House in their territory had, by her day, begun to depart from the worship of Jehovah 'to serve other gods,' it would be matter for rejoicing and thanksgiving that Ruth was once again under the protecting wings of Jehovah. The 'full reward' which Boaz wished for Ruth, was, of course, a husband to take the place of the departed Mahlon.

'Though I be not like unto one of thine handmaidens.' It should be noted that the word used by Ruth is 'Amah' which is also the Hebrew word for maiden. It is highly unlikely that this no longer young prince of the House of Ephratah, Boaz, was unmarried; he may have had daughters only and wished Ruth to 'abide here fast by my maidens' or daughters. It was the task of the

---

[22] Dean Stanley, *Sinai and Palestine,* p. 328.

young men to reap and that of the maidens to gather. To refer to oneself as 'handmaiden' or even 'servant' was in the east a formal courtesy. The marked difference which existed between the eastern and western Israelites can only be rightly understood in the light of historical fact.

Dean Stanley states: 'However much connected by vicinity and race with their western kinsmen the dwellers in Eastern Palestine have always been distinct. It has been to the main body of the people what Scotland or Ireland has been to the main course of English history. . . . The Israelite tribes who settled there hardly ever exercised any influence over their countrymen on the western banks.... This separation was, in part, owing to the great natural Tent which the Jordan has created between the two districts. . . . From first to last the eastern tribes (Reuben, Gad, and the half tribe of Manasseh) never emerged from the state of their patriarchal ancestors. . . . When on their return from the conquest of Canaan under Joshua, they reached the Jordan, the boundary between them and their more settled brethren, the western tribes, they erected, like true children of the Desert, the huge stone of division to mark the frontier, which their more civilized brethren mistook for an altar'[23] *(Joshua* 22:4-34).

The 'altar' or stone erected by these tribes ere they departed from the western side of the river Jordan, and which was mistaken by their brethren on the Canaan side for an altar of sacrifice, is clear evidence of their fear that they might eventually lose their identity with the main body of Israel. The river Jordan, the great dividing line, did tend to different habits and modes of life on each side of it, though not in worship, until the Reubenites introduced the worship of Chemosh, the god of war. With very worthy zeal the trans-Jordanic tribes made quite certain by this 'altar of witness'

---

[23] Dean Stanley, *Sinai and Palestine*, p. 323.

that their right as Israelites in future years to appear at Shiloh could not be questioned *(Joshua* 22). In the light of the above it is not surprising that Ruth, the country cousin, as it were, from Eastern Jordan should express herself as being unlike the women of Bethlehem.

No racial Moabitess would have been invited by Boaz to sit at meat with him. The Israelite of old, likewise the orthodox Jew, has always avowed to the Gentile, 'I will not eat with thee, drink with thee, nor pray with thee.' This attitude towards the Gentiles or non-Israel peoples did not arise from a supercilious superiority on the part of Israel. 'An holy nation; a chosen generation; a peculiar people; a separate people' is the decree of the Almighty which at the same time enjoined that Israel should be a blessing to all nations. Racial purity was in the forefront of all God's dealings with His chosen people.

When Ruth elected to accompany her mother-in-law on her return to Bethlehem, Naomi was faced with a new problem—a husband for Ruth. The nearest kinsman to the departed Mahlon who, according to Hebrew law, should have married the widow, Ruth, was not acceptable to Naomi as a husband for her beloved daughter-in-law. With a woman's wit, and with consummate skill, Naomi evolved a plan which met with entire success. Naomi was well aware that Boaz, on whom she had set her heart as a husband for Ruth, would not think of Ruth with a view to matrimony, while the nearer kinsman, with a prior claim, if he chose to exercise it, was still living. If this unnamed kinsman had been a desirable person, Naomi would have contacted him at once in regard to the redemption of the property and the raising up of children to Mahlon by his widow Ruth; that she was exercised lest the unnamed kinsman would claim his right to redeem is very evident from chapter 3, verse 18. Naomi set about ways and means whereby Ruth and Boaz would become acquainted with each other during barley harvest and the following wheat harvest. During all this time Ruth acted in perfect obedience to her mother-in-law, obedience which sprang from love and understanding. And when at the end of wheat harvest Naomi felt it was now time to convey to Boaz Ruth's preference for him rather than for the nearer kinsman, Naomi called for Ruth's co-operation in the delicate task. Naomi had complete confidence in her daughter-in-law, whom she knew to be a woman of great ability and strength of character; the plan which she now unfolded depended entirely upon Ruth's willingness to undertake it, and the calm and cool courage to carry it out 'Spread therefore thy skirt (Hebrew, 'thy wing') over thine handmaid; for thou art a near kinsman' (3:9). That is, 'Take me into thy protection, by taking me to be thy wife.' The allusion seems to be to a custom still observed amongst the Jews of covering the bride with the Tallith or fringed garment belonging to the bridegroom in token of his obligation to protect her. According to the sentiment of the time there was nothing immodest nor unwomanly in this bold and unusual line of action. Rightly understood it was only a gentle and delicate way of appealing to a kinsman's chivalry—and Ruth did not appeal in vain. His reply is precisely the one we should expect, 'It is true that I am thy near kinsman: howbeit there is a kinsman nearer than I ... if he will perform unto thee the part of a kinsman, well; let him do the kinsman's part: but if he will not do the part of a kinsman to thee, then will I do the part of a kinsman to thee, as the Lord liveth.' 'All the city of my people doth know that thou art a virtuous woman.' This word 'virtuous' in the Hebrew is 'chayil' and signifies force, strength of mind or body. The Septuagint reads, 'Thou art a woman of strength or power.' Boaz was not referring to any moral characteristic regarding virtue or modesty, but telling Ruth that not only he, but all the townsfolk of Bethlehem knew her to be a woman of courage and strength of purpose which had enabled her to set aside age long custom and leave her own people on the other side of Jordan to take up residence amongst them. The townsfolk would not have so approved of a woman of racial Moab.

There is no evidence that Boaz was unmarried or had not been married previously. That he was no longer young may be concluded with some degree of certainty from the fact that his mother was Rahab of Jericho fame; also in view of his words to Ruth, 'Thou hast shewed more kindness in the latter end than at the beginning' i.e., the kindness shown to Boaz in accepting him who was so much older than herself as her second husband, was greater than her previous kindness to Mahlon and Naomi. 'And now it is true I am thy near kinsman,' literally 'a goël' i.e., a kinsman-redeemer.

At the council meeting summoned by Boaz on that eventful morning at the gate of the city (the customary place for such gatherings), composed of ten of the aldermen of the city and the nearer kinsman, Ruth is not referred to as other than an Israelite. The national law of redemption was only given to Israel and only to be administered for Israelites and never to aliens.

It should be understood that Ruth was no mere chattel simply to be sold with a 'parcel of land' as it were, but a 'woman of great price' far above rubies in the eyes of those who knew her well, and a Princess of the House of Ephratah; one whose hand could only be won by a noble Prince, not only in blood and family, but also in character and life.

When Naomi decided that her husband's kinsman, Boaz, 'the mighty man of wealth' second in succession was the one she desired as a redeemer of the family property and as a husband for Ruth if the nearer kinsman would agree to relinquish his claim, she was evidently aware of the selfish character of the latter and so passed him over in favour of Boaz. The nearer kinsman would have been willing to redeem the property, but upon learning that the redemption included marriage with Ruth straightway declined, the reason being that in the event of a son being born of the union the child would be, according to Mosaic law, the inheritor of the redeemed property. The unnamed kinsman would have had no objection to redeeming the property if thereby he could perpetuate his own name on the inheritance. Boaz, by his readiness to 'mar' if need be his own inheritance and to espouse his kinsman, Mahlon's, widow, became enrolled among the ancestors of Jesus Christ, the Divine Son of Mary. This nearer kinsman was passed over, not only by Naomi, but by the Almighty in His selection of fit persons to become the ancestors of the Redeemer of Israel. The House of Ephratah, which contained within it the royal line from which presently would come the Psalmist of Israel, and of which, finally, Jesus Christ was born, was no chance affair, stained here and there by the introduction of forbidden alien blood.

This august assembly who witnessed the renouncement to redeem by the nearer kinsman now proceeded to bestow its blessing upon Boaz (4:14): 'And do thou worthily in Ephratah (the princely House of Pharez-Judah), and be famous in Bethlehem (the city).'

In their day Ezra and Nehemiah were distressed that in some instances men of Israel had married Moabite and other foreign women, and this at a time when such defection might, if ever, have been condoned on account of their captivity in a foreign land. How then did it come to pass that these Aldermen of Bethlehem welcomed this 'Moabitess' into the exclusive House of Ephratah if she were racially of the forbidden Moabites? Will it be maintained that this august assembly was not acquainted with the law in these matters? Would Ezra and Nehemiah, had they been present, have given their consent and blessing to the union of a Prince of Pharez-Judah with a woman of racial Moab? And how could Ezra and Nehemiah inflict punishment upon those of the returned Israelites who had married Moabite and other foreign women while in their midst they had Zerubbabel of the House of Pharez-Judah, Governor of Jerusalem, who would have been of sullied ancestry if, indeed, Rahab were a Canaanitess and Ruth a Moabitess. The contention that Ruth was racially a Moabitess is illogical in the light of Ezra and Nehemiah alone.

Doubtless the whole city was 'moved' over this marriage in the House of Pharez-Judah as it had been 'moved' when Naomi came home at the end of her long absence in the 'land of Moab.' With what joy would Naomi see her beloved Ruth united in marriage with this scion of the House of Pharez-Judah, a man of ability, power and wealth.

Naomi appears, to have had property of her own for she made Ruth her heir, probably by way of providing a dowry so that Ruth might enter the married state with Boaz in dignity and some affluence. All Mahlon's property would descend to Ruth's first-born child.

Ruth, by marrying Boaz, her late husband's kinsman, according to the law given by Jehovah to Israel, provided in her first-born a son and heir for the House of Ephratah which had been lacking through Mahlon, Naomi's firstborn son whom Ruth had married first.

Therefore the royal House of David is built upon this child—Ruth's first-born son. The congratulations and blessings are showered upon Naomi principally, as the maternal head of the family whose descendants would inherit the future fame and glory which would yet come to Bethlehem. This would appear to be the reason why Naomi became nurse to the child which, legally, was her son Mahlon's, 'There is a son born to Naomi' (4:17) and the inheritor of his property.

Matriarchal law is in evidence in the fact that it was Naomi and her kinswomen who named the child Obed 'serving for'—serving for an heir to Mahlon. 'And he shall be unto thee a restorer of thy life, and a nourisher of thine old age.' The child Obed was thus acclaimed an earnest of the great Kinsman Redeemer Who would, at the appointed time, be born from the royal House of David in Bethlehem; He who came 'not to be ministered unto, but to minister, and to give His life a ransom for many' *(Matthew* 20:28).

Ruth's mother-in-law by her first marriage, Naomi, and that by her second marriage, Rahab, were, with Ruth, women of outstanding character who became famous in Israel. Rahab, if still living, would have reached an advanced age when Boaz, himself no longer young, became Ruth's husband.

If Ruth lived to see her great-grandson David grow up, which in those days of general longevity is not improbable, she may have been present at his coronation at Hebron when her kinsfolk on the east side of Jordan, 'the land of Moab,' sent 120,000 men fully armed to this historic crowning. There is strong probability that Ruth was acquainted with at least some of the Psalms of David, and none could appreciate them better than she, for it was from Ruth that David, quite possibly, inherited his wonderful gift of poetry. In the sublime words of entreaty from Ruth to Naomi while yet on the east side of Jordan, the mind and soul of the poet is revealed.

It was while still in the ancestral home that David 'heard' that from Bethlehem-Ephratah the Davidic dynasty would take its rise, from which would be established 'the throne of the kingdom for ever;' and not only of his yet future election to the throne of Israel, but of the part he would take in finding 'an habitation for the mighty God of Jacob' (II *Samuel* 7:13; *Psalm* 132).

The 'horn of David' was to bud in the royal line: his enemies are those who are against the throne. This House of Ephratah from which the royal House of David was built was, as it were, the 'Holy of Holies' in the Tabernacle of David, whose course God guided from Abraham and Sarah onwards, and which eventually matured in Mary, the Mother of the Son of God.

It is beside the point to assert, as many do, that there are no racial distinctions in Christ Jesus and that the Gentiles come into the Kingdom of God in its spiritual aspect in the same way as racial Israel. That is a matter of grace and not of race. We send the Gospel message to the heathen by our missionaries, but it is significant that intermarriage with their converts is not encouraged. The evangelist with his enthusiasm and worthy zeal for conversions at home and abroad would be amongst the first to protest if an heir to the British throne were to marry a native woman of a heathen nation be she ever so soundly converted. The 'grace' would be, for the time being, completely lost sight of in the zeal for 'race.' The Almighty never confuses Race with Grace in any of His racial laws. Contrary to the received interpretation of Scripture, due to faulty apprehension of historical facts, there is no alien blood in our Lord's ancestry. The women by whom this element is supposed to have been introduced were women of Israel, specially chosen for purity of descent and spiritual qualities. Tamar, Rahab, Ruth and Bathsheba were all of Israel stock. When the chosen family of Abraham expanded into the chosen nation Israel, racial purity had premier place in the Divine commands. The chief reason for the existence of Israel at all was the preservation of a nation and within it a 'House' containing a line of Divinely-selected individuals of pure Israel descent carried on from generation to generation until finally Mary was born of that 'House,' not only racially pure but spiritually equipped to be the Mother of the Man, the Son of God, the Redeemer of Israel and the Saviour of the world. The fact should not be overlooked that Israel could only be redeemed by one of their brethren.

The generations of the House of Ephratah of Bethlehem-Judah: Pharez; Hezron; Ram; Aminadab; Nahshon; Salmon; Boaz; Obed; Jesse; David, 'And thou, Bethleem, house of Ephratha, Art few in number to be among the thousands of Juda. Out of thee shall One come forth to me, to be a Ruler of Israel; And His goings forth were from the beginning, from Eternity' *(Micah* 5:2, Septuagint).

'Blessed be the Lord God of Israel; for He hath visited and redeemed His people, and hath raised up an horn of salvation for us in the house of His servant David' *(Luke* 1:68,69).

CHAPTER 9

DEBORAH—PROPHETESS AND JUDGE
(Judges **4, 5)**

The Book of *Judges,* which records the story of Deborah, receives its title from those who, after the death of Joshua, were raised up to be the deliverers of the Israelites from their enemies. Raised up on extraordinary occasions, vested with special powers for the emergency, the judges delivered the nation from some pressing danger and their power generally terminated with the crisis which had brought them forth.

Hostility to the Israelites dated from the days of Joshua who soon after his entry into the Promised Land subdued the Northern Canaanites, slew their king, Jabin, and burned his city of Hazor to the ground. The Israelites were commanded to have no dealings with these Canaanites because of the diseases from which they suffered, diseases induced by their wickedness and because their religion was of a licentious nature.

In the period of the Judges which succeeded Joshua, ever and anon the Israelites sinned and ever and anon when they cried to God they were delivered from their enemies.

The fourth of the judges, Deborah, holds first rank among the illustrious women mentioned in the Scriptures: she freed Israel from the yoke of the Canaanite and ruled them during forty years with as much glory as wisdom.

A French writer has observed that the Bible, which has not hidden the failings of the Patriarchs, the mistrust of Moses and Aaron, the imprudence of Joshua, the fall of David and the follies of Solomon, has recorded nothing of Deborah but her hymns and prophecies, her victories and her laws.[24]

We are told very little about Deborah as a person; she was married to a chieftain named Lapidoth, and lived in a pleasant spot in Mount Ephraim in a house overshadowed by palm trees. It seems that she was made a Judge in Israel because of her outstanding ability and because of her gift of prophecy. 'It was this gift of being able to look into the future and accurately to predict coming events which lifted Deborah out of the general run of women and gave her influence in a sphere wider than her own household; she was a poet with a gift as spontaneous as Moses or David, and as the event proved she was also something of an astronomer. But it is not as a prophetess or as a poet that Deborah takes her place in Israel history, it is as the person who instigated and organized the campaign that ended the twenty years' tyranny which Jabin, the Canaanite king of Hazor, exercised over the tribes.'[25]

Deborah used her great influence and gifts to rouse the people in a time of despair and confusion to withstand the encroaching Canaanites under their king, Jabin, a grandson of the Jabin whom Joshua slew; the city of Hazor had been rebuilt and the Canaanite army greatly increased. Not only did Jabin continuously harass the Israelites but his commander-in-chief, Sisera, was as a sleuth-hound in pursuing and capturing the women of Israel to rob them of their beautiful double-embroidered garments (embroidered on both sides) and hand the maidens over to his soldiers.

Deborah, as she sat in Mount Ephraim to judge the people and heard their distress, decided upon a course of action to free them from the Canaanite oppressor. She sent for Barak, Prince of Issachar, the general of the Israel forces and put before him a

---

[24] P. le Moigne. Quoted by Matilda Betham, *Celebrated Women,* p. 314.
[25] N. Lofts, *Women in the Old Testament,* p. 75.

proposal to go to war against the Canaanites. Barak hesitated to undertake the expedition with his small army. Jabin was reputed to have 30,000 footmen, 3,000 horsemen and 900 chariots of iron,[26] a formidable army. Deborah was adamant, confident that God would give Israel the victory. Barak replied, 'If thou wilt go with me, then I will go: but if thou wilt not go with me, then I will not go.' The reason for this condition was that in ancient Israel it was the custom for a prophet or high-standing priest to accompany the armies to the battlefield to bless and to encourage in the name of the Lord. The people of Israel had so departed from God, practising the sins of the heathen, that religion was at a low ebb and neither priest nor prophet could be found to accompany the armies. Barak flatly refused to go unless Deborah, a prophetess and woman of saintly character, consented to accompany him. Deborah consented but not without a warning. Together they went down to Barak's headquarters at Kadesh (where was also a sanctuary, the word Kadesh signifying 'holy'), and there they laid their plans. First, messengers were sent across the river Jordan to urge the tribes of Reuben, Gad and the half tribe of Manasseh to come to their aid against the Canaanites. These tribes hesitated to leave the security of their homes on the east side of Jordan although they did have a conscience in the matter; in the end they refused to leave their pastoral life and the care of their flocks to fight the battles of their western brethren. Deborah and Barak had no greater success with the seafaring tribes of Dan and Asher. Dan chose to abide by his ships, probably many of the tribe were on the high seas, and Asher preferred to remain in his ports where he carried on a flourishing import and export trade. Four and a half tribes had refused their assistance in this time of distress and turmoil in Israel. The northern tribes of Issachar, Napthali and

---

[26] Josephus, *Antiq.*, Bk. V, Chap. V.

Zebulon responded willingly as did also the tribes of Ephraim, Benjamin and the other half tribe of Manasseh. Judah and Simeon do not appear to have been summoned; possibly they needed to defend their own territory against the Canaanites of the south.

Deborah appears to have given the order for battle and for procedure for she directed Barak to dispose his men on the slopes of Mount Tabor while the mighty host of the Canaanites assembled on the Plain of Esdraelon beneath. The Plain of Esdraelon has seen more fighting than any other part of Palestine: situate in the centre of Palestine it is ideal fighting ground in dry weather but in rain or storm quickly becomes a swamp; also the winding river Kishon which runs alongside and has many rivulets running into it rapidly overflows its banks. Deborah announced to Barak that she herself would go up to the top of Mount Tabor and, at a given word of command from her, Barak and his men would rush down the mountain and join issue with the Canaanites on the plain beneath. The summit of Mount Tabor is flat, about a mile in circumference and commands magnificent panoramic views of all Palestine. Here Deborah took up her position. Day after day the prophetess anxiously scanned the skies; at length her patience was rewarded with the first indication of the annual shower of meteors which occurs in Palestine in November. Deborah had learned from observation that the meteoric display was followed by storms of rain and sleet; she therefore with marvellous strategy, upon the first sign in the heavens, gave the order to Barak, 'Up; for this is the day in which the Lord hath delivered Sisera into thine hands: is not the Lord gone out before thee? So Barak went down from Mount Tabor, and ten thousand men after him.' As they swiftly descended the mountain the storm broke, rain and hail driven by an east wind blinded the oncoming Canaanites across the plain, which rapidly became a quagmire in which the chariot wheels stuck and the hoofs of the terrified horses were broken. The Israelites rushing down the mountain had the storm on their backs and were sheltered to a great extent by the mountain. The plain beneath soon presented a fearful scene of destruction, the river Kishon overflowed its banks and those who fell by the sword of the Israelites were swept away by the raging torrent. Sisera saw at once the defeat of his army and descending from his chariot fled away on foot north-eastwards to a small colony of Kenites where he believed he would be safe from the pursuing Israelites. The story is well-known of Sisera's reception at the tent of Jael, wife of Heber, prince of the Kenites: upon making request for a drink the Canaanite Commander-in-chief was given a preparation of goat's milk, known as leben; it is highly soporific and soon the warrior was fast asleep. The Scripture narrative adds 'that Jael gave Sisera butter in a 'lordly dish.' This was the 'prince's bowl,' a beautiful and costly dish found in every house of any standing and kept for important visitors; no doubt Sisera noted with satisfaction that he was thus honoured.

'When the children of Israel entered the Promised Land, the children of the Kenite, Moses' father-in-law, went with them from Jericho into the land of Judah, at the south, and settled there. But Heber removed his tent from there and was living far to the north, near the southern extremity of (what was later called) the sea of Galilee. The encounter with Sisera took place at the western part of the plain of Jezreel, or Esdraelon, by the river Kishon, and Sisera fled north-eastwards to the tent of Jael for shelter and protection, arriving, perhaps, three days after the battle. The effrontery of it! A man out capturing women is in danger of being captured, and runs to a woman for protection!

'He would have probably captured Jael herself, at another time if he could. She knew this very well. The House of Heber was at peace with Jabin, Sisera's king, but that is not saying Jael was at peace with Jabin or Sisera, for women were very independent in those days, and only a treacherous woman loses the sense of loyalty towards her sex. Sisera stood a suppliant at the door of Jael's tent while Barak was in hot pursuit. It is not likely that Jael recognized him at the moment, but she would under the circumstances be filled with fear lest an armed warrior meant mischief to herself; and realizing that the giving of the hospitality he desired meant her own safety, while the refusal of that hospitality meant peril, bade him welcome and when he asked for water gave him milk.

'Once inside, his quick request for her to stand at the door and tell a lie when his enemy came—she an unarmed woman and he a warrior armed to the teeth, would arouse her suspicions; she probably then realized who this man was, Sisera the despoiler of the women of Israel—Israel with whom the Kenites from the days of Moses, had had a most sacred Covenant; among whom in fact the Kenites dwelt as guests (I *Samuel* 15:6).

'She hesitated no longer. He had thought to entrap her by the Arab custom of desert hospitality, which carries the promise of protection with the giving of food. Fired with indignation at once she dispatched him by the only means she had at hand. Barak now stands at the tent door, but too late. Jael has the honour of slaying the enemy. And a few miles away a woman of fashion and of folly is saying to the women of her train, "Have they not found, have they not divided the spoil? A damsel, two damsels to every man?" Commentators have wrangled over the question whether Jael ought not to have obeyed that custom of Arab hospitality and spared Sisera. Jael knew better than to transgress a covenant made with God's people for the sake of man-made custom.'[27]

---

[27] Katherine Bushnell, *God's Word to Women,* para. 649.

Deborah celebrates this victory of two women over a capturer of women in a song which knows no rival for beauty in Hebrew literature. The Song of Deborah is pronounced by scholars the most remarkable specimen of Hebrew poetry in the Bible: but, 'The closing part of Deborah's song has justly been regarded as a specimen of poetical representation that cannot be surpassed.'[28]

The song was evidently composed for a victory parade or festival for Prince Barak, their general, and the troops have their part along with Deborah, as made clear by Ferrar Fenton in his translation of the Bible in modern English *(Judges* 5).

THE SONG OF DEBORAH

DEBORAH:

'For free freedom in Israel,
You heroes and people bless the Lord.'

BARAK:

'Let kings hear, let princes listen,
I, to the Lord, myself will sing;
I chant to the Ever-Living God of Israel.'

THE TROOPS:

'Lord, in Your advance from Sair,—
In Your march thro' the field of Edom,—
The earth shook, the heavens poured down,
The storm clouds poured out water!
The mountains melted before the Lord;
Sinai itself before the Living God of Israel!'

DEBORAH:

'In the days of Shamgar, son of Anath,
In the days of Yal the caravans ceased,

---

[28] Cassell in Lance's Commentary on Authorized Version.

And travellers went in the bye-paths,—
Judges ceased—in Israel ceased,—
Till I, Deborah, arose,—
Till I arose, a mother to Israel!'
BARAK:
'They chose for themselves new gods!—
When there was war at the gates,
Was a shield or a spear to be seen,
In forty thousand of Israel?'
DEBORAH:
'My heart can picture Israel!—
Heroes among the people bless the Lord!'
THE TROOPS:
'You riders upon white asses,—
And you who dwell in the plain,—
And the travellers by roadways publish,
With the sound as of rushing waters,
The kindness the Lord has done;
The kindness to Israel's hamlets,
When the Lord's force rushed down to the dales!'
BARAK:
'Arise! arise you! Deborah!
Awake, awake! and utter a song!'
DEBORAH:
'Arise, Barak, and conquer,—
Conqueror, son of Abinoam!
Let the Nobles and People descend;
The Lord sent me to summon heroes:
Come to me, Ephraim, rooted in Amalek;
Follow me, Benjamin, from your caves;
Come to me, Makir, with your chieftains;

With Zebulon wielding the writer's pen,
And Issakar's eloquent Princes;—
And along with Issakar, Barak,
Who directs the march with skill.
My heart aches for Reuben's absence;—
Why stayed he among the sheepfolds,
To hear the cries of his flocks?
My heart aches for Reuben's absence!
Ghilad remained beyond the Jordan;—
But why stayed Dan in his ships?
And Ashur rest on the shore of the sea,
And continue to lie in his ports?
Zebulon's men risked their lives to death,
With Naphthali from the highlands.'
BARAK:
'Kings came out to the war,
Like Canan's Kings at Thanak,
Who fought by the Brook of Megiddo:—
They took no silver as plunder;—
The stars, they fought from the skies,—
The stars from their high course fought against Sisera!—
The river Kishon swept them away,
That ancient river—the river Kishon!'
DEBORAH:
'Rush strongly along, my life!
How the hoofs of the horses sound,
With their mighty leapings and prancings!
"Curse Meroz," said the man of the Lord,
"When cursing, curse its people,—
For they came not with help to the Lord,
To help the Lord and His heroes!"

But bless the children of Jael,—
The wife of Heber the Kenite,
Bless all the sons of her tent.
He asked her water,—she gave him milk!
She offered him butter on a beautiful (lordly) dish!
Then she stretched her hand to the nail,
Her right hand to the workman's hammer,—
And Sisera pierced through his head,
And broke, and drove through his temples!
At her feet he bowed,—fell down,—
When he bowed, he fell down dead!'
THE TROOPS:
'Sisera's mother, at the evening hour,
Bent and watched from her window;—
"What prevents his chariot's return?
What delays the tramp of his chargers?"
Her wise women answered to her,—
Nay, continued her words to herself,—
"Have they not found plenty of plunder?
A lovely girl for the generals,
And a plunder of robes for Sisera?
A plunder of robes embroidered,—
Embroidered robes for the necks of the victors?"
DEBORAH, BARAK AND TROOPS:
'Lord! thus destroy Your foes:—
But let Your friends march on,
Like the sun in his glory'[29]

And the land had rest for forty years.

---

[29] Ferrar Fenton's Translation.

In Deborah's Song, verse 4, the natural elements of storm used by the God of Israel for the destruction of the Canaanites is a reminder to the people of the same elements used which their ancestors experienced at Sinai.

The roads had become unsafe, the Israelites kept to bypaths because of their enemies, even the caravans ceased. 'Judges ceased . . . till I, Deborah, arose, a mother in Israel.' This word 'mother' means, according to Semitic usage, in this connection 'female chief'—a female ruler in Israel.

Deborah complains (v. 8) that when Israel entered the Promised Land, forty thousand armed men marched before them; now, not a spear or a shield had been lifted to defend Israel against Sisera. 'Riders upon white asses' (v. 10). Princes and the nobility were distinguished by the white asses which they invariably rode. 'You who dwell on the plain,' a term for the leisured classes; some translators have 'you who sit on rich carpets.' The 'travellers by roadways,' i.e. the common people. Thus all classes are called upon to speak of the kindness of the Lord to Israel. 'The stars in their courses fought against Sisera' (v. 20). Deborah here refers to the annual shower of meteors which guided her in ordering the battle which resulted in so singular a victory over the enemy. The Canaanites were terrified by the meteoric display.

It is Deborah herself who sings the praises of Jael and asks the God of Israel to

'Bless the children of Jael,—
The wife of Heber the Kenite,
Bless all the sons of her tent.'

According to Jewish tradition Deborah and Barak died about the same time and were buried in the same tomb at Kadesh where a national monument was erected to their memory. This monument stood to within a few centuries of the present era.

CHAPTER 10

JEPHTHAH'S DAUGHTER *(Judges 11:30-40)*

T he ninth judge in Israel, Jephthah, is recorded as the son of a harlot; in like manner Jeroboam is so recorded in the Septuagint, while the Authorized Version has, 'son of a widow woman;' it was unfortunate that the alternative translation, 'widow woman,' recognized in some Eastern languages, was not given in the case of Jephthah's mother. His father, Gilead, appears to have married as his second wife a widow who, dying before her son Jephthah grew up, left him at the mercy of his step-brothers and sisters. Driven cruelly from his father's house Jephthah became, through adversity, a great soldier and leader of men with the additional quality of loyalty to Jehovah.

The Israel tribes on the east of the river Jordan have been regarded by the historian as less civilized than their western brethren and yet these trans-Jordanic tribes produced some outstanding characters, valiant chiefs and national heroes. The grandest and the most romantic character that Israel ever produced, Elijah the Tishbite, came from the forests of Gilead as did Jephthah.

Jephthah, an outcast from his father's house, became the leader of a band of freebooters. The eastern Israelites, long oppressed by the Ammonites and aware of his reputation for valour, begged that he would become their captain and lead them against the enemy.

Jephthah, animated of God, levied an army on the east of Jordan; as he prepared for battle he rashly vowed that if the Lord should grant him success he would devote or sacrifice whatever should first meet him from his house.

'If thou shalt without fail deliver the children of Ammon into mine hands, then it shall be, that whatsoever cometh forth of the doors of my house to meet me, when I return in peace from the children of Ammon, shall surely be the Lord's, and I will offer it up for a burnt offering.' In the Ferrar Fenton translation the word 'burnt' does not appear and according to the *People's Bible Encyclopedia* the words could equally well be translated, 'shall surely be the Lord's, or I will offer a burnt offering.' A misunderstanding of the nature of the vow caused the spread of the story in the East that Ipheginea, the daughter of Jephthah, had been sacrificed. To arrive at the truth of the matter it should first be remembered that Jephthah, a Judge in Israel, was well acquainted with the law and having made his vow in the presence of the Lord was aware that the vow could be fulfilled by a person devoted to the service of God or by a burnt offering. Dr. Adam Clarke, the distinguished Bible Commentator, refutes the popular idea that Jephthah's daughter was sacrificed; she was merely dedicated to the Tabernacle service with a burnt offering and this is all Jephthah's vow implied.

The victorious Jephthah, on his return home, was met by his daughter, his only child, 'behold, his daughter came out to meet him with timbrels and with dances.' Her father realized what a terrible sacrifice it would be to give her over to the service of the Tabernacle and to perpetual virginity in fulfilment of his vow—which also meant parting from her forever. The faith of the young woman is seldom taken into account when considering her story; she was God-centred rather than self-centred and instead of reproaching her father helped him to see the necessity for fulfilling his vow, 'My father, if thou hast opened thy mouth unto the Lord, do to me according to that which hath proceeded out of thy mouth; forasmuch as the Lord hath taken vengeance for thee of thine enemies, even of the children of Ammon. And she said unto her father, Let this thing be done for me: let me alone two months, that I may go up and down upon the mountains, and bewail my virginity, I and my fellows.' The word virginity signifies 'separation' and so the daughter of Jephthah, with her friends who also were dedicated and about to relinquish the life of the world to devote their lives to the service of God, spent the next two months in freedom and fellowship, 'And it came to pass at the end of two months, that she returned unto her father, who did with her according to his vow which he had vowed.' The daughters of Israel, probably many relatives, came yearly to celebrate or praise her celibacy, the word 'lament' here, according to Gesenius, really meaning 'praise.' The R.V. says 'celebrate.'

St. Paul (*Hebrews* 11:32) extols Jephthah among the heroes of Israel. Had he been guilty of human sacrifice, which was 'an abomination unto the Lord,' the Apostle would not have included him among those who 'through faith subdued kingdoms, wrought righteousness ... of whom the world was not worthy.'

CHAPTER 11

HANNAH (I *Samuel* 1, 2)

There are many instances in the Old Testament where a man possessed two wives; not, however, in every instance is volitional polygamy implied, for according to the Mosaic law a man must take his brother's widow to wife whether he were already married or not. It is not possible to state whether the case of Elkanah was such. In the Scripture narrative we learn that Elkanah was a Levite of Mount Ephraim; that he had two wives, Hannah and Peninnah. The former was extremely pious and greatly beloved of her husband but the latter, who had children, upbraided Hannah with her lack of them.

As Elkanah and his whole family attended one of the solemn feasts at Shiloh, from his share of his sacrifices he gave Peninnah and her children portions, but to Hannah he gave the best part of the peace-offering, 'a worthy portion' of the Passover lamb which fell to his share.

At these feasts it was Peninnah's common practice to reproach Hannah with her lack of children. Hannah, at last, took it so ill that she refused to eat. Elkanah, to comfort her, told her that his deep affection for her was better than ten sons.

Hannah, still in distress of mind, entered the Tabernacle and prayed with intense fervour for a child and vowed to surrender him as a Nazarite for life, to the service of God. The old priest, Eli, sitting at the door of the Tabernacle, observing her imploring attitude in prayer, on hearing her case, gave her his blessing and wished that the Lord might grant her request. Hannah again became cheerful and returned to her home Divinely impressed that God would grant her request. 'And Eli answered and said, Go in peace: and the God of Israel grant thee thy petition that thou hast asked of him. And she said, Let thine handmaid find grace in thy sight. So the woman went her way, and did eat, and her countenance was no more sad' (I *Samuel* 1:17, 18).

In the following year, when the Passover was again to be celebrated, Hannah had a little son whom she named Samuel, which means, 'asked of the Lord.' After she had weaned the child and he was about three years' old Hannah carried him to Shiloh and took with her three bullocks and one ephah of flour and a bottle of wine and presented him before the Lord and put him under Eli's tuition. And she said, 'Oh my lord, as thy soul liveth, my lord, I am the woman that stood by thee here, praying unto the Lord. For this child I prayed; and the Lord hath given me my petition which I asked of Him: therefore also I have lent him to the Lord: as long as he liveth he shall be lent to the Lord.'

On this occasion—the presentation and dedication of Samuel to the Lord—Hannah composed a song celebrating the holiness, greatness, wisdom, power and mercy of God.

'And Hannah prayed, and said, My heart rejoiceth in the Lord, mine horn is exalted in the Lord; my mouth is enlarged over mine enemies; because I rejoice in thy salvation. There is none holy as the Lord: for there is none beside thee: neither is there any rock like our God. Talk no more so exceeding proudly; let not arrogancy come out of your mouth: for the Lord is a God of knowledge, and by Him actions are weighed. The bows of the mighty men are broken, and they that stumbled are girded with strength. They that were full have hired out themselves for bread; and they that were hungry ceased: so that the barren hath born seven; and she that hath many children is waxed feeble. The Lord killeth, and maketh alive:

He bringeth down to the grave, and bringeth up. The Lord maketh poor, and maketh rich: He bringeth low, and lifteth up. He raiseth up the poor out of the dust, and lifteth up the beggar from the dunghill, to set them among princes, and to make them inherit the throne of glory: for the pillars of the earth are the Lord's, and He hath set the world upon them. He will keep the feet of His saints, and the wicked shall be silent in darkness; for by strength shall no man prevail. The adversaries of the Lord shall be broken to pieces; out of heaven shall He thunder upon them: the Lord shall judge the ends of the earth; and He shall give strength unto His king, and exalt the horn of His anointed.'

The Hebrew word 'Jehovah' of the Old Testament and from the Septuagint Greek version can be identified with the New Testament name 'Lord.' The Hebrew word 'Anointed,' that is 'Messiah,' is identical with Christ. The name 'Jesus' of the New Testament is identical with Joshua in the Old Testament—the One Who leads into the Promised Land of rest from all our enemies. Eve bestowed on Him the title 'Lord;' Hannah first called him 'the Anointed,' that is 'Christ,' and the Virgin Mary was instructed to name Him, before He was born, Jesus. These names were bestowed upon Him by three holy women of old, prophetesses of God—Eve, Hannah and Mary.

In her Song, Hannah brings in the resurrection, the 'horn' or power of the Lord, and prophesies the preservation of the nation: 'He will keep the feet of His saints.'

Hannah's gift of song was inherited by her son Samuel, the last of the Judges and the founder of the schools of the prophets, who taught his young prophets, whom he had in training, to praise the Lord in song. Dean Payne-Smith says, 'One of that choir (of the prophet Samuel) was Heman, the son of Joel, Samuel's first-born, who there acquired that mastery of music which made him one of the three singers selected by David ... to arrange and preside over the Temple service. Blessed with a numerous family, who all seem to have inherited Samuel's musical ability, he trained them for song in the house of Jehovah, with cymbals, psalteries and harps, and it is remarkable that no less than fourteen of the twenty-four courses of singers were Samuel's own descendants, and that as long as the first Temple stood they were the chief performers of that psalmody which he had instituted.[30]

'God gave to Heman fourteen sons and three daughters' (I *Chronicles* 25:5). And if as Dean Payne-Smith says, 'Psalmody commenced with that hymn of triumph sung by Miriam and the women on the shores of the Red Sea with timbrel and dance,' it was, as pointed out by Mrs. Bushnell,[31] introduced into the Temple service by the Song of Hannah, taken up by Samuel and his female descendants, as well as his male, through Heman and extended through the days of Ezra and Nehemiah by both women and men; also the mention of 'women-singers' and the description of a religious procession in *Psalm* 68:25 is clear evidence that women had an important part in the psalmody of the Temple. Hannah might be termed the Mother of Psalmody in the Temple and with those other gifts which she possessed, gifts of prophecy and grace, Hannah, the Mother of Samuel, towers above the women of her day.

---

[30] *Prophecy a Preparation for Christ.*
[31] *God's Word to Women,* paras. 783, 784.

CHAPTER 12

ABIGAIL (I *Samuel* 25)

It is believed that through the covetousness of her parents Abigail was married to Nabal, a man of great wealth but of a churlish disposition withal and a drunkard.

Nabal was a prince of the tribe of Judah, a descendant of Caleb, son of Jephunneh, one of the two spies who were permitted to see the Promised Land and to have inheritance therein. One of Caleb's grandsons was named Ziph and the descendants of this grandson were known as Ziphites. Ziph had his settlement in Canaan close to Caleb's inheritance in the Hebron country. Nabal belonged to the House of Ziph and by Josephus is called a Ziphite.

Abigail, whose name signifies 'a father's joy,' was also of the tribe of Judah, a descendant of one of the Judah families who settled around Carmel; possessions in this country caused Nabal and Abigail to be known as Carmelites and it is possible that as Abigail was known as the Carmelitess she was a chieftainess in her own right.

Nabal's immense wealth appears to have been derived from numerous flocks of sheep and goats which had their pastures south of Carmel, near Maon.

David, in his exile, lurked in the neighbouring wilderness of Paran. His men not only did no hurt to Nabal's flocks, but protected them from the Arabs and wild beasts, and assisted the herdsmen in every possible way.

When Nabal held his shearing-feast David in very polite language sent to desire a present from his kinsman of whatever part of the provision he pleased. Nabal, in the most harsh and surly manner, told David's messengers that he knew better things than to give his servants provisions to a fellow who had run away from his master to his partisans. Apart from his natural churlishness there was another reason why Nabal subjected David to so humiliating treatment. Nabal, as a prince of Judah, had been brought up in the belief that the future king of Israel would come from that tribe, and he was well aware that David was a scion of the House of Caleb-Ephratah of the royal line from Pharez-Judah. But, to the satisfaction of the cynical Nabal, Saul of the tribe of Benjamin had been elected King; hence he sought to wound David's feelings by referring to Saul as his master and in this way seeking to disparage David's importance as a prince of Judah and by saying to the messengers, 'Who is David? 'and 'Who is the son of Jesse?' It was this insult, rather than the refusal of the food of which he and his band of followers stood in need, which aroused David's wrath and caused him to swear to exterminate every person in the House of Nabal.

'When the messengers hastened back to David and told him how they had been received David lost no time. He immediately armed and equipped four hundred of his men and set forth upon the road to give the egregious Nabal a lesson in manners. Meanwhile, one of Nabal's servants who had seen what had happened reported the whole incident to Abigail, Nabal's lovely and intelligent wife. He told her how well David's men had treated them, how boorish Nabal's behaviour had been, and expressed his fears as to the vengeance that David would take. They would all suffer for Nabal's rudeness, but what was to be done for, as he put it, 'he is such a son of Belial, that one cannot speak to him.' Abigail does not appear to have resented this description of her husband and acted with commendable promptitude. She took two hundred loaves, two bottles of wine, five sheep ready dressed, five measures of parched corn, a hundred clusters of raisins, and two hundred cakes of figs. This substantial gift she put on the backs of asses and, without saying a word to Nabal, set forth with them in the direction of David's camp. When therefore David, cursing Nabal and swearing to destroy him and his whole household, was advancing in the direction of Carmel, he found himself suddenly met by a train of heavily-laden asses conducted by serving-men and, riding at the head of them, a beautiful woman.

'She, on seeing him, immediately dismounted and, falling at his feet, addressed him eloquently, not seeking to excuse her husband but roundly condemning him, and explaining that all would have been different if she had been allowed to see David's emissaries herself. She also recognized David as the future ruler of Israel and intimated with exquisite tact that both for the present and for the future it would be wise to avoid entanglement in a blood feud with a powerful person like Nabal. She begged him therefore to accept, as a peace offering, the present that she had brought.

'David was deeply moved by her eloquence and beauty. He also appreciated the sound sense of her words. It was terrible to think that she might have been among the victims of his vengeance, and he thanked the Lord for having kept him from hurting her. He accepted the gift which she had brought and bade her go in peace.

'When she returned home she found a tremendous feast in progress, and Nabal very drunken. She wisely refrained from telling him her news that night. It could not, however, be kept from him for, avaricious as he was, he would soon ask for the supplies that were missing. On the following morning, therefore, when Nabal was feeling far from well, Abigail gently informed him of all that had happened. She had expected an outburst of fury, but fortunately the anger that Nabal felt was too much for him. The result was a stroke that rendered him speechless and paralysed, and in ten days he was a dead man.'[32]

Nabal, upon hearing from Abigail the account of her meeting with David and her conversation with him, realized the seriousness of the offence he had caused to the man who, in spite of appearances would one day be ruler in Israel. It was this shock more than any of his enormities which hastened Nabal's demise.

Abigail's address to David not only disarmed his rage but procured his highest esteem for her virtue and her wisdom; her faith in God and in the fulfilment of prophecy on his behalf moved him deeply.

'And (Abigail) fell at his (David's) feet, and said, Upon me, my lord, upon me let this iniquity be: and let thine handmaid, I pray thee, speak in thine audience, and hear the words of thine handmaid. Let not my lord, I pray thee, regard this man of Belial, even Nabal: for as his name is, so is he; Nabal is his name, and folly is with him: but I thine handmaid saw not the young men of my lord, whom thou didst send. Now therefore, my lord, as the Lord liveth, and as thy soul liveth, seeing the Lord hath withholden thee from coming to shed blood, and from avenging thyself with thine own hand, now let thine enemies, and they that seek evil to my lord, be as Nabal. And now this blessing which thine handmaid hath brought unto my lord, let it even be given unto the young men that follow my lord. I pray thee, forgive the trespass of thine handmaid: for the Lord will certainly make my lord a sure house; because my lord fighteth the battles of the Lord, and evil hath not been found in thee all thy days. Yet a man is risen to pursue thee, and to seek thy soul: but the soul of my lord shall be bound in the bundle of life with the Lord thy God; and the souls of thine enemies, them shall He sling out, as out of the middle of a sling.

---

[32] Duff Cooper, *David*, p. 83.

And it shall come to pass, when the Lord shall have done to my lord according to all the good that He hath spoken concerning thee, and shall have appointed thee ruler over Israel; that this shall be no grief unto thee, nor offence of heart unto my lord, either that thou hast shed blood causeless, or that my lord hath avenged himself: but when the Lord shall have dealt well with my lord, then remember thine handmaid. And David said to Abigail, Blessed be the Lord God of Israel, which sent thee this day to meet me: and blessed be thy advice, and blessed be thou, which hast kept me this day from coming to shed blood, and from avenging myself with mine own hand. For in very deed, as the Lord God of Israel liveth, which hath kept me back from hurting thee, except thou hadst hasted and come to meet me, surely there had not been left unto Nabal by the morning light (so much as one man child) (R.V.)' (I *Samuel* 25:24-34).

It is said by some Bible students that it is impossible to trace the source of Abigail's information with regard to David's future greatness, and that it may have been derived from Samuel or from one of his students at the school of the prophets. But Abigail did not have to go beyond her own home for this information, for if she were not aware of the prophecies concerning the House of Bethlehem-Ephratah to which David belonged she would learn of them after her marriage to Nabal. Abigail believed these covenant promises and in God's faithfulness to appoint David 'a sure house' and to make him ruler over Israel: 'The soul of my lord shall be bound in the bundle of life with the Lord thy God'—these words have reference to temporal security as well as to the blessing of God Almighty upon David as king.

'When the news was brought to David (of Nabal's demise) he was delighted to hear it. It was long since he had met anyone so beautiful as Abigail, and her intelligence was remarkable. She had made a deep impression upon him during their short interview, and her faith in his future made him feel that she would not be unwilling to share it.

'He therefore sent to her a proposal of marriage which she immediately accepted. She returned with the messengers which he had sent and brought with her five ladies; one of them was as pretty as herself, and came from an equally honourable family. Her name was Ahinoam and, with Abigail's cheerful consent, David married both of them. The three lived in complete harmony, and it was Ahinoam who first produced an heir for David, to whom he gave the name Amnion.'[33]

Significantly, the number five occurs in the story of Abigail: five sheep ready dressed; five measures of parched corn and five ladies who accompanied her when she came to David for, according to the science of numerology, the number five signifies 'Divine Grace.'[34] In this connection it is interesting to note that the Israelites came out of Egypt in ranks of five and that the number five was an abomination to the Egyptians.

Again, when under Joshua they took possession of the Promised Land, the vanguard from the eastern side of Jordan passed over the river marshalled in fives. Thus were the Israelites given the seal of 'Divine Grace' or 'Divine Strength' for the fulfilling of God's purposes in the world.

[33] Duff Cooper, *David*, p. 84.
[34] See Dr. E.W. Bullinger, *Number in Scripture*, Part 2.

CHAPTER 13

BATHSHEBA (II *Samuel* 11, 12)

The seventh daughter, as the name Bathsheba signifies, of Eliam, son of Ahithophel and wife of Uriah, the Hittite, has been recorded in history as having been married to a foreigner. On this point it cannot be too emphatically stated that in ancient Israel it was the custom to take the name of the conquered country, and as the Hittites were among the nations to be driven out of Canaan the Israelites would take the name of the people they supplanted and the territory they conquered. Thus Uriah the Israelite would become known as Uriah the Hittite because he lived in what was at one time Hittite territory. The mysterious empire of the Hittites had by Joshua's day dwindled to a few unimportant colonies: in Canaan they were confined to a small area in southern Judea and were eventually driven out.

In this way David's bodyguard who were all of Israel bore names of foreign and heathen people.

Uriah is a Hebrew name signifying 'Jehovah is light,' a name not likely to be found among a heathen people.

The Hittites were an ugly people, with yellow skins, whose mongoloid features are faithfully represented both on their own monuments and on those of Egypt. They were squat and stout; their eyes were dark and their black hair they wore in pigtails. No racial Hittite would have been accepted as a husband for the beautiful Bathsheba, of the House of Israel.

While Bathsheba's husband, Uriah, was employed at the siege of Rabbah she happened to bathe herself in her garden; David espied her from the roof of his adjacent palace and sent for her. Bathsheba had little option but to obey the king's command. David's sin with her was made blacker still when he procured the death of her husband Uriah. When this foul deed was accomplished David made the widow his wife. The fact that Bathsheba was granddaughter of Ahithophel may explain his defection from David.

'To David Bathsheba seemed not only the most beautiful but by far the most intelligent woman he had ever known. She was clever and ambitious. She was determined to please him and to prove the companion whom he had always sought in vain. She sincerely loved him as a man—it was difficult not to—and she loved him the more for being king. She had been brought up on the fringe of the court. From her earliest years she had heard little but court gossip: and high position at court had always been presented to her as the goal of man's endeavour, the highest reward that merit could obtain. Her grandfather had been held out to her as an example of all that was admirable and he had himself impressed upon her young mind the importance of worldly success. She had therefore, believing in her own capabilities, resented her enforced marriage with an officer who was never likely to rise high in his profession or to occupy any influential post. Ahithophel had insisted upon it and his word was law to the whole family so that it was useless to protest. Now she suddenly found herself raised to a pinnacle of power, whence it seemed that she could control the fate of Ahithophel himself, and come near to ruling the whole kingdom. It was a high test of character but Bathsheba kept her head. . . . David himself found it difficult to believe that there could be great evil at the root of so much good. For he was happy as he had never been, having in one person the wife whom he adored, the counsellor whose advice he respected and the sweet companion of whom he was never weary. His relations with God were of so intimate and close a character that he could not feel happy if he thought that God was angry. Conversely, he could not believe that God was angry when he felt so supremely happy. The laws of religion were not so hard and fast as they came to be at a later period. They had been very fluid in the days of the patriarchs, and had permitted much that future generations would condemn. He himself was no ordinary man, and he knew it, and the ordinary rules need not apply to his every act. . . . The part Bathsheba had to play in public was easy, for custom laid down in the minutest particulars the forms of mourning which a widow was required to observe. So long as these were carried out correctly, nobody was concerned as to the degree of sincerity that underlay the conventional acts. . . . Nor was there anything surprising in the fact that when the period of mourning was completed the king should cast his eye upon the beautiful young widow and take her into his household as one of his many wives. Public comment was therefore not aroused, and if there was some private whispering it was almost entirely confined to court circles.

'All these things might indeed so easily have happened in the natural course of events that there were moments when David could almost persuade himself that they had done so, and could forget the terrible message that he had sent to Joab (11:15). But there were other moments when the sense of guilt was heavy upon him. He was accustomed to discuss with his God all matters that closely affected him. He would take to God the problems that puzzled him, and would usually obtain assistance in solving them; he would complain to God bitterly when he met with misfortune, and would thank God from his heart when all went well. But in his communings with God this matter of Uriah was never mentioned.

'It was the business of the prophets to know everything, and it was not long before the whispers of the court reached their ears. The two principal prophets at this period were Gad and Nathan. The latter was the younger of the two and the one whom David preferred. He, in turn, deeply loved his master, whose complex character he understood and admired. Nathan thought it his duty to ascertain the true facts upon which the rumours that reached him were based. When he knew all he felt that he should approach David, for he could see that the king was unhappy, and he knew that he would remain so as long as he refused to admit to himself or to God that he had done grievous wrong.

'Nathan knew to its depths the generous and compassionate heart of David, and he knew also that he had only to touch that heart in order to correct the moral obliquity which was the cause of his mental distress. Nothing throws a more revealing light upon the true beauty of David's character than the story which Nathan from his intimate knowledge of the man invented in the certainty of the effect it would produce.

' "There were two men," so he began, "in one city; the one rich, and the other poor. The rich man had exceeding many flocks and herds: but the poor man had nothing, save one little ewe lamb, which he had bought and nourished up: and it grew up together with him, and with his children; it did eat of his own meat, and drank of his own cup, and lay in his bosom, and was unto him as a daughter. And there came a traveller unto the rich man, and he spared to take of his own flock and of his own herd, to dress for the wayfaring man that was come unto him; but took the poor man's lamb, and dressed it for the man that was come to him."

'Before Nathan had finished speaking, David, who had been seated, sprang to his feet, his eyes blazing with indignation.

' "As the Lord liveth," he exclaimed, "the man that hath done this is worthy to die: and he shall restore the lamb fourfold, because he did this thing, and because he had no pity." Then Nathan, rising also and gazing with stern and sorrowful eyes upon the king, said in a low voice that David long remembered, "Thou art the man."

'Like one walking in darkness suddenly arrested by a dazzling light shining into his eyes, David remained staring at the prophet who in a few sentences showed the similarity of his conduct towards Uriah to that of the rich man in the parable. When he had ended David had only these words to say, "I have sinned against the Lord". . . .

'Nathan knew when David had confessed his sin that his penitence came from the depths of his being, and that he would never again be guilty of such an act. Passionately he prayed for forgiveness:

' "Wash me throughly from mine iniquity
And cleanse me from my sin.
For I acknowledge my transgression
And my sin is ever before me.
Against thee, thee only, have I sinned,
And done this evil in thy sight."

'When he had largely eased his mind of remorse and when he could begin to believe that the sincerity of his repentance had earned forgiveness, the child who had been born to Bathsheba fell seriously ill. David felt for all his children the most tender affection, and this one, the first-born of the woman whom he loved the best, had already won his heart. When, therefore, it was stricken by disease he was in despair. For several successive days he would not eat, nor drink, nor wash, but continued in unremitting prayer for the child's life. When at the end of a week the child died his servants dared not break the news to him. While the child was still alive and there was hope, he behaved like one distraught, and they therefore dreaded what the effect might be when they told him that all was over. But he read the news in their frightened faces and asked them calmly, "Is the child dead?" And when they, trembling, replied that it was so, he immediately rose from his knees "washed and anointed himself, and changed his apparel." He then worshipped in a normal manner, and on his return sat down to a meal.

'His servants were astonished at such unconventional behaviour, and the bolder among them asked him to explain it.

' "What thing is this that thou hast done?" they enquired, "Thou didst fast and weep for the child, while it was alive; but when the child was dead, thou didst rise and eat bread."

'He replied, sadly and coldly, "While the child was yet alive, I fasted and wept: for I said, Who knoweth whether the Lord will not be gracious to me, that the child may live? But now he is dead wherefore should I fast? Can I bring him back again? I shall go to him, but he shall not return to me." To Bathsheba David remained devoted until the end; and she proved that perfect companion whom he had missed so long and found at last. Another son was born to her, to whom was given the name of Solomon.

'And the Lord loved him; and he sent by the hand of Nathan the prophet, and he called his name Jedidiah, because of the Lord.'[35] The name Jedidiah given to the child Solomon by Divine command signifies "Pardoned by the Ever-Living."[36] This token of Divine mercy was received by the chastened David with fervent expressions of gratitude, reflected in many of his Psalms, notably the fifty-first Psalm.

Bathsheba bore yet three other sons, Nathan, Shimea and Shobab; she was extremely careful in the education of her sons,

---

[35] Duff Cooper, *David*.
[36] II *Samuel* 12:24, 25. Ferrar Fenton translation.

particularly of Solomon, concerning whom many promises had been made.

David became aware in after years that Bathsheba was his Divinely-appointed wife and would have been his in God's own time; this awareness made his sin appear yet more heinous, though it also brought home to him a realization of the tender mercy and forgiveness of his Lord.

And now David the king is an old man and about to quit this earthly sphere. There is much plotting and intrigue at court in connection with his successor. One of his sons, Adonijah, hopes by swift action, ere his father departs, to have the crown placed upon his own head. Bathsheba, however, had the solemn promise from David that the crown of Israel should descend to her son Solomon.

Upon the advice of Nathan, the prophet, her friend and counsellor, she sought an audience of the king, when she reiterated his promise of the crown to Solomon. When she left the king's apartment Nathan entered to confirm her words. Then the aged King, roused to indignation, upon hearing of Adonijah's attempted usurpation, said to the prophet, 'Call me Bathsheba.' When his beloved wife re-entered the apartment and stood before the King he uttered the words which put all her fears at rest: 'As the Lord liveth, that hath redeemed my soul out of all distress, even as I sware unto thee by the Lord God of Israel, saying, Assuredly Solomon thy son shall reign after me, and he shall sit upon my throne in my stead; even so I will certainly do this day. Then Bathsheba bowed with her face to the earth, and did reverence to the king, and said Let my Lord king David live forever' (I *Kings* 1:28-31).

It has been said of Bathsheba that she never performed a single action under the thrust of her own impulse; never uttered a word which was not put into her mouth by some man. This criticism is but the result of scanty historical records. Bathsheba, the mother of

Solomon, was instrumental in obtaining the throne for him and because of her the temple at Jerusalem bore Solomon's name, not David's.

Bathsheba would be the most honoured woman at Solomon's coronation; it was indeed a proud moment for her when the crown of Israel was placed upon his head.

According to Jewish tradition Bathsheba composed and recited the thirty-first chapter of *Proverbs* to her son Solomon upon the occasion of his marriage to the daughter of Pharaoh.

Bathsheba is one of the four women mentioned in the Scriptures as ancestresses of our Lord and who, when they were brought into the royal enclosure in the House of Judah, were widows.

CHAPTER 14

THE QUEEN OF SHEBA (II *Chronicles* 9:1-12)

This picturesque queen of ancient history, whose correct title was Queen of Saba, was ruler of the Sabeans, a people distinct from the Ethiopians and Arabs; it was a custom among them to have women for their sovereigns in preference to men. Her name the Arabs say, was Belkis; the Abyssinians, Maqueda.[37] Our Lord referred to her as 'the queen of the south' without mentioning any other name, but gives His sanction to the truth of the expedition.

This famous royal lady was an Israelite, traditionally called a Jewess, but whether her ancestors of the tribe of Judah emigrated from Egypt or Palestine, it is impossible to say; she was yet a worshipper of the Lord God of Israel although Sabaism, the worship of sun, moon and stars, was the religion of her country and of all the East and a constant stumbling-block to the Israelites.

How large a following of Israelites the Queen had in her own country is not now known but evidently it was sufficient to allow of the worship of the God of Israel without let or hindrance.

There are many instances in history of an Israelite of the tribe of Judah settling in a foreign country, and with that Divine gift for rulership which marked this tribe becoming, with his followers, the dominant party and in time occupying the throne.

Solomon, who in her day sat upon the throne of Israel, had announced his intention of building a great Temple at Jerusalem, in the course of which his servants travelled in many directions to

---

[37] James Bruce, *African Travels*, Vol. I, p. 110.

collect material. Southern Arabia was famous for almug trees or sandalwood and gold, the gold of Ophir, a district of south-east Arabia, being greatly prized. When the emissaries of Solomon came to Southern Arabia for supplies of timber, gold and precious stones the Queen may have heard from them of the great wisdom of the King of Israel. Herself a person of learning and that kind of learning which was peculiar to Palestine, she could not believe that these were other than exaggerated stories which she heard, and determined to test the truth of these reports for herself; she would take the long journey to Jerusalem and try her kinsman Solomon with 'hard questions.' Solomon had the reputation of solving theological enigmas or parables in which he had been instructed by Nathan the Prophet. It was, therefore, theological rather than philosophical questions which she wished to put to her kinsman Solomon; there was, however, no question too hard for Solomon for 'he knew more than all men of the orbits of the planets, of the origination of light, and fixed sustaining systems, and the results of the revolving spheres, and his fame was spread among all the nations around' (I *Kings* 5:11-12, Ferrar Fenton translation).

From her home at Saba, or Azaba on the Arabian Gulf, the Queen came to Jerusalem, a distance of 1,500 miles, under the protection of Hiram, King of Tyre, whose daughter is said, in the forty-fifth Psalm, to have escorted her into Solomon's Court. She went not in ships nor through certain parts of Arabia for fear of attack by Ishmaelites and was escorted by shepherds, her own subjects, to Jerusalem and back again, making use of her own country vehicle, the camel—her own camel a white one of prodigious size and exquisite beauty.[38] In Israel royal personages and the nobility rode on white camels or asses.

The Queen of Sheba's arrival at Jerusalem was made a state

---

[38] James Bruce, *African Travels,* Vol. I, p. 122.

occasion. Solomon received his kinswoman with every mark of respect and honoured her at his Court.

'And when the queen of Sheba heard of the fame of Solomon she came to prove him with hard questions. And she came to Jerusalem with a very great train, with camels that bare spices, and very much gold, and precious stones: and when she was come to Solomon, she communed with him of all that was in her heart. And Solomon told her all her questions: there was not anything hid from the king, which he told her not. And when the queen of Sheba had seen all Solomon's wisdom, and the house that he had built, and the meat of his table, and the sitting of his servants, and the attendance of his ministers, and their apparel, and his cupbearers, and his ascent by which he went up unto the house of the Lord; there was no more spirit in her. And she said to the king, It was a true report that I heard in mine own land of thy acts and of thy wisdom. Howbeit I believed not the words, until I came, and mine eyes had seen it: and, behold, the half was not told me: thy wisdom and prosperity exceedeth the fame which I heard. Happy are thy men, happy are these thy servants, which stand continually before thee, and that hear thy wisdom. Blessed be the Lord thy God, which delighted in thee, to set thee on the throne of Israel: because the Lord loved Israel for ever, therefore made He thee king, to do judgment and justice. And she gave the king a hundred and twenty talents of gold, and of spices very great store, and precious stones: there came no more such abundance of spices as these which the queen of Sheba gave to king Solomon' (I *Kings* 10:1-10).

We are indebted to the Queen of Sheba for so graphic a description of the splendour of King Solomon's Court and the ascent by which he went up to the house of the Lord. The word 'ascent' would have been better translated 'causeway' as elsewhere in the Scriptures. This roadway from Mount Zion where was the King's palace and across the valley of Hinnom to Mount Moriah on the opposite hill where stood the newly-erected Temple was evidently a great feat of engineering skill—probably a winding road with many retaining walls—to have excited the wonder and admiration of the much-travelled queen of Sheba. It is said that Solomon caused all the roads in and around Jerusalem to be paved with black basalt brought from the eastern shores of the Dead Sea.

Apparently the Queen of Sheba came to Jerusalem with the idea of impressing the King of Israel with her own splendour, wealth and learning, for when she came to his Court and beheld so much greater magnificence and wisdom than her own, 'there was no more spirit in her.' The reports she had heard, so far from being exaggerated stories, were underestimates of Solomon's glory and scientific knowledge; her spontaneous confession to Solomon of his greater glory and wisdom reveals the nobility of her character.

But above all her motives for coming to Jerusalem one stands out in high relief; we are told that it was 'concerning the name of the Lord' that this queen came to consult Solomon. To the theological questions which she put to the King she received the enlightenment which she desired. The Queen of Sheba's confidence in the Lord God of Israel to fulfil His covenant with Abraham is strikingly borne out in her words, 'because thy God loved Israel, to establish them forever.' This is by no means the language of a pagan but of a person skilled in the ancient history of Israel.[39]

The Scripture record of the visit of the Queen of Sheba to the king of Israel ends with the simple statement, 'She turned and went to her own country, she and her servants.'

A wealth of legend has grown around this famous royal visit to the entire obscuration of the germ of truth in the tradition which

---

[39] James Bruce, *African Travels,* Vol. I, p. 112

lies buried beneath.

The territory of the Queen of Sheba included the land on the opposite shores of the Red Sea from Arabia, Ethiopia or Cush, now known as Abyssinia, derived from the Arabic name Habesh; there was also another Ethiopia to the east of Arabia, known at that time as Cush, as shown on ancient maps.

According to the law of her country the reigning sovereign must be a woman; therefore the Queen of Sheba could not be succeeded by her son. It was probably on the advice of King Solomon that the Queen of Sheba decided to make her son Viceroy, or Governor, on the opposite shores of the Red Sea, for on her return to her capital, Azaba, she sent her son to Jerusalem to be trained in rulership. This task was faithfully carried out by the King of Israel and upon the completion of the young man's training in governorship Solomon had the Queen of Sheba's son ordained and anointed Viceroy of Ethiopia in the Temple at Jerusalem, and the name Menelik bestowed upon him which signifies, 'to set up and ordain.' The young man, being of the Israel faith, Solomon sent with him a number of high-standing priests and a large following of Israelites, chiefly of the tribe of Judah, so that the newly-appointed Governor entered upon his duties in dignity and with the support of the influential King of Israel.

Also with Menelik came many Doctors of the Law, particularly one of each tribe to make judges in the kingdom from whom the present Umbares or Supreme Judges derive, three of whom always attend the king; and with these came also Azarias, son of Zadok, the High Priest who brought a Hebrew transcript of the Law.[40]

In time this governorship became a dynasty which continues in

---

[40] ibid, p. 113.

Abyssinia to the present day; also the descendants of the Israelites who came with Menelik remain a distinct though greatly impoverished people, practising a corrupt Hebrew religion, and known as the Falasha.

The female succession continued in the Arabian territory down to, at least, New Testament times, for we read of Candace, Queen of the Ethiopians (another of the Arabian titles) whose steward, a man of great authority at her Court and an Israelite who had come up to Jerusalem to worship; his meeting with Philip, the Evangelist, and his conversion and baptism, are recorded in the eighth chapter of the *Acts of the Apostles.*

It is said that the name Candace denotes 'royal authority' and was commonly given to the queens of Meroe in Ethiopia. It is certain that Kanadah in the Abyssinian language signifies a governor. Pliny says that the government of Ethiopia subsisted for several generations in the hands of queens named Candace. It is said that by the preaching of her eunuch, the queen, Candace, was converted to the Christian faith.

The Queen of Sheba's visit to King Solomon received lasting fame and approval from our Lord's references to this event. Addressing the Pharisees who had gathered around Him our Lord made several references to well known events in Israel history, one of which was relating to the Queen of Sheba: 'The queen of the south shall rise up in the judgment with the men of this generation, and condemn (convict) them; for she came from the utmost parts of the earth to hear the wisdom of Solomon; and, behold, a greater than Solomon is here' (*Luke* 11:31). This is one of our Lord's few recorded references to the resurrection.

Our Lord never would have brought in the name of this great queen if the charge of immorality could have been levelled against her; nor would the Pharisees, who were well versed in their ancient history, have tolerated hearing this queen held up to them as an example had her character been besmirched in the manner we are so glibly told today.

How meticulously correct was our Lord's reference to her as 'the queen of the south,' for from Jerusalem looking south, it is an almost straight line to Southern Arabia. And again, how precise is His description, 'the utmost parts of the earth,' for again looking south the land surface ends where Southern Arabia is joined by the sea.

CHAPTER 15

HULDAH THE PROPHETESS (II *Kings* 22)

In the days of Solomon's son the whole body politic of Israel was changed by the secession of ten tribes and, having with them the birthright tribe of Ephraim they retained the name, House of Israel. Two tribes only, Judah and Benjamin, remained loyal to the throne of David, and were known as the House of Judah. Henceforth the history of these two Houses was separate and distinct. The House of Israel was taken captive in *c.* 725 BC; 140 years earlier than the final downfall of the House of Judah. The prophecies concerning the restoration and expansion of the House of Israel have been amply fulfilled; the prophecies concerning the partial restoration of the House of Judah have been fulfilled and await the final stage when the House of Israel and the House of Judah will again become one nation. 'And I will set up one shepherd over them, and he shall feed them, even My servant David; he shall feed them, and he shall be their shepherd. And I the Lord will be their God, and My servant David a prince among them' *(Ezekiel* 34:23, 24).

'And there shall be one fold, and one shepherd' *(John* 10:16).

In the reign of Josiah, called 'the faithful,' last king of Judah prior to the captivity, when all but a few in the nation had forgotten God and the teaching of Moses, a general repair and restoration of the Temple of Jerusalem was ordered by the king, himself a good man who 'walked in all the paths of his ancestor David, and did not turn to the right or left' (Ferrar Fenton translation).

While this important work was in progress a book was found

by Hilkiah the High Priest which proved to be the 'original Book of the Law . . . the autograph copy engraved by Moses and placed in the Ark' (Ferrar Fenton Notes).[41] Hilkiah handed the book to Shaphan the scribe, saying, 'I have found the book of the law in the house of the Lord[42] . . . and Shaphan the scribe told the king, saying, Hilkiah the priest hath delivered me a book. And Shaphan read it before the king.

'And it came to pass, when the king had heard the words of the book of the law, that he rent his clothes. And the king commanded . . . Go ye, inquire of the Lord for me, and for the people, and for all Judah, concerning the words of this book that is found: for great is the wrath of the Lord that is kindled against us, because our fathers have not hearkened unto the words of this book, to do according unto all that is written concerning us.'

So Hilkiah the priest went to Huldah the prophetess, the wife of Shallum, keeper of the wardrobe, and communed with her. This Shallum was a man of dignity and of an eminent family. His wife, Huldah, was well known for her piety and gift of prophecy. Some translations have 'she dwelt in Jerusalem in the college;' 'she dwelt in Jerusalem in the second rank of the Levites,' and 'she dwelt in Jerusalem in the second quarter.'

When the deputation from Josiah, the king, came to her 'she said unto them, Thus saith the Lord, the God of Israel: Tell ye the man that sent you to me.

'Thus saith the Lord, Behold, I will bring evil upon this place, and upon the inhabitants thereof, even all the words of the book which the king of Judah hath read. Because they have forsaken Me, and have burned incense unto other gods, that they might provoke me to anger with all the work of their hands; therefore My wrath shall be kindled against this place, and it shall not be quenched. But

---

[41] Now believed to have been the Book of *Deuteronomy*.
[42] Josephus, *Antiq.*, Bk. X, Chap. IV.

unto the king of Judah, who sent you to inquire of the Lord, thus shall ye say to him, Thus saith the Lord, the God of Israel: As touching the words which thou hast heard, because thine heart was tender, and thou didst humble thyself before the Lord, when thou heardest what I spake against this place, and against the inhabitants thereof, that they should become a desolation and a curse, and hast rent thy clothes and wept before Me; I also have heard thee, saith the Lord. Therefore, behold, I will gather thee to thy fathers, and thou shalt be gathered into thy grave in peace, neither shall thine eyes see all the evil which I will bring upon this place. And they brought the king word again' (R.V.).

So great was the esteem in which Huldah, the prophetess was held, that the high dignitaries of the Temple and the Royal Court came to her to obtain light upon God's Law.

It is perfectly clear that women were admitted to the highest office of teaching, that of prophets, and that Huldah was the wisest prophet of the times. To her the deputation from the king came to learn whether the book they had found was really the 'Law of the Lord.' The revelation of God given her led to national reform and revival of religion.

Schroeder remarks in his Commentary, 'Prophecy was a gift of the Spirit and as being so had no restriction as to sex.'

If the question be asked, 'What is it to prophesy in the biblical sense of the word?' the answer must be, 'To speak for God.'[43]

Huldah was one of the great and wise women of her day, used of God for the reproof and reform of His people Israel, and whose name in the nation was never forgotten. It was the ideas and views of a later age when woman had lost much of her dignity which led Luther to express the opinion, 'No gown worse becomes a woman than to be wise.'

---

[43] Katharine Bushnell, *God's Word to Women,* para. 778.

The prophecy of Huldah was literally fulfilled; the reform carried out by Josiah was of short duration, and after his death all the evil foretold by Huldah overtook the nation, and the House of Judah was led away into captivity.

CHAPTER 16

QUEEN ESTHER (Book of *Esther*)

The Apostle Paul in his second letter to Timothy states: 'All Scripture is given by inspiration of God, and is profitable for doctrine, for reproof, for correction, for instruction in righteousness' (3:16), and so every Book that God has written has a Divine Idea which it is our business to discover and to study; it will thus become obvious that the Book of *Esther* is inserted in our Holy Scriptures for the purpose of 'instruction in righteousness.'

The late Rev. Dr. Pascoe Goard pointed out that the Book of *Esther* is the story of the final drama in the history of the Amalekites and that the story begins actually in the Book of *Numbers* where the utter destruction of the Amalekites is foretold. In the destruction of the House of Haman and the contemporary Amalekites this prophecy was fulfilled.

The story belongs to the captive House of Judah and is one of the very few we possess which tell of the conditions under which the tribes of Judah and Benjamin lived in the land of strangers.

When Jeconiah, king of Judah and grandson of the good king Josiah, was taken captive to Babylon he had in his *entourage* a man of the tribe of Benjamin named Kishai, a typical Benjamite name. This man's grandson was Mordecai and it would seem that this Benjamite family continued to fill posts of distinction at the Court of Nebuchadnezzar as they had at the Court of Judah. When the Babylonian empire was conquered by the Persians Mordecai was granted a post at the Court of Ahasuerus.

The identity of Ahasuerus has puzzled commentators and

students of the Scriptures and on this point no agreement has been reached. Ferrar Fenton, however, in his translation of the Scriptures has unwittingly given the clue to the identity of Ahasuerus.

Among the Persians Ahaz was a title meaning king. The personage of history who liberated the House of Judah was, as we know him, Cyrus. Ferrar Fenton gives the more correct spelling and pronunciation of his name Kerosh, and sometimes Khushrush. This name is spelt and pronounced according to the nationality of the person recording his history and so in the Hebrew we have Ahashuerus or King Kerosh, while his throne name was Artaxerxes and under his throne name much of his history was recorded.

This discovery opens up the Book of *Esther* in a wonderful way and makes much that was obscure more easily understood.

This Cyrus, or Keros, or Ahaz Kerosh or Ahasuerus conquered the Babylonian Empire and so had under his rule many races.

To celebrate his victory Cyrus gave a great feast lasting eighty days. It was a Persian custom to unite great councils with great festivities and this celebrated feast was carried out with more than usual Oriental splendour.

Towards the end of the feast the supreme Queen, Vashti, was summoned by the king to appear before the assembled guests. Vashti signifies simply 'beauty' and was not her real name, which was said to be Amestris. The king sent his seven chamberlains to conduct Vashti in state into his presence, and with that disregard for the rights of others which marked Eastern potentates Cyrus expected his command to be obeyed forthwith; no small consternation was caused at Court when Vashti refused to appear. The king himself was 'wroth' and consulted the seven princes who were his counsellors as to the steps which should be taken to punish Vashti for this flagrant act of disobedience. Something must be done, but it must be according to law. As the law then stood a wife could be divorced for disobedience and the same law must apply even were the wife a queen, and so Vashti was deposed in the third year of the reign of Cyrus.

Cyrus appears to have taken little notice of the Jewish captives in his conquered territory and does not appear to have been acquainted with their appearance as distinct from his other subjects. The king readily acquiesced in the suggestion of his counsellors that another wife should be found to replace Vashti, and so from all the provinces of his kingdom young women were brought to be prepared and trained in Court etiquette, that from among them the king might choose one to take Vashti's place.

Mordecai, the Benjamite, had brought up a young cousin, Hadassah, which name signifies 'myrtle,' 'that is, Esther, his uncle's daughter: for she had neither father nor mother, and the maid was fair and beautiful; whom Mordecai, when her father and mother were dead, took for his own daughter.' On her mother's side Hadassah was of the royal House of Judah.[44]

To the dismay of Mordecai, this beloved young cousin was among the maidens chosen to be prepared for the king's palace. In parting with Hadassah, one of Mordecai's many injunctions to her was that she should not 'shew her people nor her kindred.' Probably with this in view it was Mordecai himself who changed her name from the Hebrew Hadassah to the Persian Esther—a star—and so the myrtle that bloomed in the Hebrew home became a Star to shine in the Persian palace.

Soon, Esther found favour with Hegai, the governor of the women's quarters. Mordecai, in deepest concern for the fate of his

---

[44] Josephus, *Antiq.*, Bk. XI, Chap. VI.

beloved young kinswoman, paced before the court of the women's quarters every day 'to know how Esther did, and what should become of her.' It was only as a court official himself that Mordecai dared to venture on to the forecourt of the women's quarters. Not yet were Esther and Mordecai aware that their separation and association with the Persian monarch was part of the Divine plan for the liberation of their people.

Esther's exaltation was soon to be announced. Once the beautiful young Hebrew woman appeared before Cyrus the king, her fate was sealed: none but she had the remotest chance of becoming 'Queen of Queens.'

'Esther had not yet shewed her kindred nor her people; as Mordecai had charged her: for Esther did the commandment of Mordecai, like as when she was brought up with him.' And Mordecai also was honoured for he was promoted at Court and 'sat in the king's gate' as one of the king's counsellors. On the occasion of his marriage to Esther, Cyrus 'made a great feast unto all his princes . . . even Esther's feast,' a feast in her honour which was marked by a release of prisoners and remittance of tribute.

The description of this feast corresponds to the statements of ancient Persian luxury and magnificence which the Greek authors have sent down to us, and which they state to have been remarkably evinced in their banquets. Their sumptuousness in this respect became proverbial. The vast numbers of persons entertained at their great feasts, as well as the long continuance of these feasts, are points noted by ancient writers.

The advancement of Mordecai at the Court of Cyrus was a source of annoyance and jealousy to the Prime Minister, Haman, the Agagite, friend and counsellor of the king, and who, much in the royal favour, induced Cyrus to issue a command that his more exalted status should be acknowledged by the people, and that he should receive from them that reverence and popular worship which he craved. Haman was exceedingly mortified to find that Mordecai, whom he had discovered to be a Jew, would take no part in this popular homage and worship of the Prime Minister.

Mordecai would not bow because it involved religious homage and this he was not prepared to give to any but the Lord God of Israel. Haman's mind became filled with ideas of revenge and, scorning to lay hands on Mordecai, he resolved to have the whole race of the Jews in the Persian territories exterminated.

Representing to Cyrus that 'There is a certain people scattered abroad and dispersed among the people in all the provinces of thy kingdom; and their laws are diverse from all people; neither keep they the king's laws: therefore it is not for the king's profit to suffer them. If it please the king, let it be written that they may be destroyed: and I will pay ten thousand talents of silver to the hands of those that have the charge of the business, to bring it into the king's treasuries. And the king took his ring from his hand, and gave it unto Haman, the son of Hammedatha the Agagite, the Jews' enemy. And the king said unto Haman, The silver is given to thee, the people also, to do with them as it seemeth good to thee. Then were the king's scribes called on the thirteenth day of the first month, and there was written according to all that Haman had commanded unto the king's lieutenants, and to the governors that were over every province, and to the rulers of every people of every province according to the writing thereof, and to every people after their language; in the name of king Ahasuerus (Cyrus) was it written, and sealed with the king's ring. And the letters were sent by posts into all the king's provinces, to destroy, to kill, and to cause to perish, all Jews, both young and old, little children and women, in one day, even upon the thirteenth day of the twelfth month, which is the month Adar, and to take the spoil of them for a prey. The copy of the writing for a commandment to be given in every province was published unto all people, that they should be ready against that day. The posts went out, being hastened by the king's commandment, and the decree was given in Shushan the palace. And the king and Haman sat down to drink; but the city Shushan was perplexed' (3:8-15).

Mordecai, with consternation, read this decree of the king and 'rent his clothes, and put on sackcloth with ashes.' Queen Esther, in the seclusion of the palace heard of it from her maids and her chamberlains. 'Then was the queen exceedingly grieved,' and she sent one of the king's chamberlains to Mordecai with a request for further particulars of the threatened disaster to their people. Mordecai had already declared himself to be a Jew and now it was necessary that Esther also should declare her race at Court.

The Persians at that time had the most wonderful postal system in the world and from Shushan, 'The City of the Lily,' the decree of death to the Jewish people throughout the Empire was being prepared. Hatach, the king's chamberlain, deputed to wait upon Esther, was the medium by which the Queen communicated with her cousin, Mordecai, outside the palace, and now to convince Esther of the desperate situation of the Jewish people, Mordecai 'gave him the copy of the writing of the decree that was given at Shushan to destroy them, to show it unto Esther, and to declare it unto her, and to charge her that she should go in unto the king, to make supplication unto him, and to make request before him or her people. And Hatach came and told Esther the words of Mordecai. Again Esther spake unto Hatach, and gave him commandment unto Mordecai; All the king's servants, and the people of the king's provinces, do know, that whosoever, whether man or woman, shall come unto the king, into the inner court, who is not called, there is one law of his to put him to death, except such to whom the king shall hold out the golden sceptre, that he may live: but I have not been called to come in unto the king these thirty days. And they told to Mordecai Esther's words. Then Mordecai commanded to answer Esther, Think not with thyself that thou shalt escape in the king's house, more than all the Jews. For if thou altogether holdest thy peace at this time, then shall there enlargement and deliverance arise to the Jews from another place; but thou and thy father's house shall be destroyed: and who knoweth whether thou art come to the kingdom for such a time as this? Then Esther bade them return Mordecai this answer, Go, gather together all the Jews that are present in Shushan, and fast ye for me, and neither eat nor drink three days, night or day. I also and my maidens will fast likewise; and so will I go in unto the king, which is not according to the law: and if I perish, I perish. So Mordecai went his way, and did according to all that Esther had commanded him' (4:8-17).

It is instructive to observe how little the heart of Esther was changed by her elevation to the throne. As an Israelite she believed it to be a principle in the Divine government that whenever a child of God occupies a position by the appointment of Providence it is that he (or she) may there perform some specific work for God.

It seemed to Mordecai also that the strange life of Esther was designed by Providence to effect the safety of the Israel of God: 'Who knoweth whether thou art come to the kingdom for such a time as this.'

The answer of Esther to Mordecai's appeal was one that, manifesting Esther's piety, must have greatly comforted him. It is evident from the words of Esther that her maidens also were of her own race, otherwise they could not have united with her in fasting and in prayer to the Lord God of Israel.

'Now it came to pass on the third day, that Esther put on her royal apparel, and stood in the inner court of the king's house, over against the king's house: and the king sat upon his royal throne in the royal house, over against the gate of the house. And it was so, when the king saw Esther the queen standing in the court, that she obtained favour in his sight: and the king held out to Esther the golden sceptre that was in his hand. So Esther drew near, and touched the top of the sceptre. Then said the king unto her, what wilt thou, queen Esther? and what is thy request? It shall be even given thee to the half of the kingdom. And Esther answered, if it seem good unto the king, let the king and Haman come this day to the banquet that I have prepared for him.'

It was a custom of the Persians to grant requests at banquets, and so Queen Esther invited the King and his Prime Minister Haman to a banquet. On the night prior to the banquet 'could not the king sleep,' and calling for the Court chronicles and having the latest records read to him it was found that Mordecai had rendered signal service to the king by discovering and revealing a plot by two of the king's chamberlains, Bigthan and Teresh, to take the life of the king. And the king said, 'What honour and dignity hath been done to Mordecai for this?' And his servants answered, 'There is nothing done for him.' The Persians had an order called 'Orongae,' or 'Benefactions of the King;' men who had rendered signal service were duly and sometimes extravagantly rewarded.

The King and Haman came in state to the banquet which Queen Esther had prepared. Though a king ate alone, his guests were allowed to take wine with him afterwards, and this was the moment when requests were made.

The request of Queen Esther was a large one in face of an unalterable decree; the king, however, in granting her request found a way out of the difficulty: the decree could not be reversed but an antidote was provided; the Jews were allowed to act on the defensive and so the force of the decree was broken. The king honoured Mordecai as the saviour of his life and the relative of his queen, Esther, by making him Prime Minister instead of the wicked Haman who ended his life on the gallows which he had prepared for Mordecai.

In the homes of the Jews sorrow and fear of coming destruction was replaced by joy and gladness and the exchange of presents. A memorial feast was instituted to be known for all time as the 'Feast of Purim;' not only was the deliverance to be remembered but those religious acts by which it was preceded.

Not only was Queen Esther, at the peril of her life, instrumental in the deliverance of her people but also by her noble conduct and prayers effecting a change of heart in her husband Cyrus. The heathen king became a true follower of the Lord God of Israel, thus fulfilling the prophecy of Isaiah:

'Who calls His Shepherd, Cyrus,
Who will effect My plans;
Who Jerusalem will rebuild,
And found a Temple there!
Thus saith the Lord to His Messiah,
To Cyrus, whose right hand He wields . . .
Who called your name, am Israel's God,
For Jacob's sake, My friend,
And Israel's, whom I chose
I call you by your name,
To an Office you know not.'[45]

This was foretold of Cyrus one hundred and forty years before

---

[45] *Isaiah* 44:28; 45:1, 4, Ferrar Fenton translation.

the Temple at Jerusalem was demolished. Cyrus was called God's Shepherd by Xenophon as well as by Isaiah.

When Esther's husband, Cyrus, read the prophecy of Isaiah, he declared: 'Thus saith Cyrus the King: Since God Almighty hath appointed me to be king of the habitable earth, I believe that he is that God which the nation of the Israelites worship; for indeed He foretold my name by the prophets, and that I should build Him a house at Jerusalem, in the country of Judea.'[46]

It is recorded that when Cyrus read the prophecy 'and admired the Divine Power' an earnest desire seized upon him to fulfil what was so written '. . . Cyrus also sent back to Jerusalem the vessels of gold which king Nebuchadnezzar had pillaged out of the Temple, and had carried to Babylon.'

As instance of the complete change in Cyrus, the onetime heathen potentate, he declares in his decree giving the Jews liberty to return to Palestine and to rebuild the Temple at Jerusalem; 'I permit them to have the same honour which they were used to have from their forefathers. . . . The priests shall also offer these sacrifices according to the laws of Moses in Jerusalem; and when they offer them, they shall pray to God for the preservation of the king and of his family, that the kingdom of Persia may continue.'[47]

The inventory of the Temple treasures was put into the hands of Cyrus; the king passed it on to his treasurer and at the same time gave order for their return to Jerusalem, 'The whole of them were carried by Shashba-zar with the returning transports from Babel to Jerusalem.'

It is recorded that Cyrus died in peace in Persia but whether Esther or Vashti was the mother of the heir to the throne is not recorded. That Cyrus died before his queen is practically certain for Esther and Mordecai were entombed in the same spot in

---

[46] Josephus, *Antiq.*, Bk. XI, Chap. I.
[47] ibid.

Hamadan.

The Jewish people have never forgotten the debt they owe to the great Queen Esther: the feast of Purim is kept up to this day and the story of their deliverance which her noble and courageous action, together with the deep piety and reliance on the Lord God of Israel to save His people, evinced by both herself and Mordecai, is recited at this annual feast.

Sir John Malcolm in his *Sketches on Persia,* tells us that the sepulchre of Esther and Mordecai stands near the centre of the city of Hamadan. It is a square building terminated by a dome, with an inscription in Hebrew upon it, translated and sent to him by Sir George Gore Ouseley, late Ambassador to the Court of Persia. It is as follows: 'Thursday, fifteenth of the month Adar, in the year 4474 from the creation of the world was finished the building of this temple over the graves of Esther and Mordecai, by the hands of the good-hearted brothers, Elias and Samuel, the sons of the deceased Ishmael of Kashan.'

In a description of the interior Sir R.E. Porter states, 'On passing through the little portal which we did in an almost doubled position, we entered a small arched chamber in which are seen the graves of several rabbis. Having trod lightly by their graves a second door of such very small dimensions presented itself at the end of this vestibule that we were constrained to enter it on our hands and knees, and then, standing up we found ourselves in a larger chamber to which appertained the dome. Immediately under its concave stand two sarcophagi, made of a very dark wood, carved with great intricacy of pattern and richness of twisted ornament, with a line of inscription in Hebrew running round the upper ledge of each. The Sarcophagi were rescued from the ruins of the first edifice at its demolition by the Tartars and preserved on the same sacred spot.'

Dr. J.E. Polak, formerly physician to the late Shah of Persia, gives similar information in his work, *Persia:* 'The only national monument which the Jews possess in Persia is the tomb of Esther at Hamadan, the ancient Ecbatana whither they have made pilgrimage from time immemorial. . . . In the entrance hall which has but a low ceiling are recorded the names of pilgrims; also the year when the building was restored. Then one gains entrance to a small four-cornered chamber in which there are two high sarcophagi made of oak which are the monuments of Esther and Mordecai. On both of them are inscribed in Hebrew the words of the last chapter of the Book of *Esther* as well as the names of three physicians at whose expense the tomb was repaired' (p. 26).

The last chapter of the Book of *Esther,* with the last verse of the previous chapter, states:

'And the decree of Esther confirmed these matters of Purim; and it was written in the book. And the king Ahasuerus (Cyrus) laid a tribute upon the land, and upon the isles of the sea.

'And all the acts of his power and of his might, and the declaration of the greatness of Mordecai, whereunto the king advanced him, are they not written in the book of the chronicles of the kings of Media and Persia? For Mordecai the Jew was next unto king Ahasuerus (Cyrus), and great among the Jews, and accepted of the multitude of his brethren, seeking the wealth of his people, and speaking peace to all his seed.'

In this connection Professor Upham, in his *Wise Men* (p. 117), observes: 'In the historical cycles of the ancient world, wherever the centre of power is, there the Hebrew is sure to be, and sure to draw to himself the chief interest. So it is on the shores of the Nile, by the rivers of Babylon and in the palace of the great King in Sushan. With this people the true interest of history begins; and it seems ordained that it shall never afterwards be wholly separated from them. The predestined end of the culture of the Greeks was reached when Hebrew evangelists and apostles made their language imperishable.'

Queen Esther stands out in ancient history as a great Hebrew woman who 'wrought her people lasting good' and provided that 'example in righteousness' which the descendants of her race, the English-speaking people, ever tend to follow.

CHAPTER 17

THE VIRGIN MOTHER

The prophecy of Isaiah, 'Behold, a virgin shall conceive, and bear a son, and shall call His name Immanuel' (7:14), is the Word of God written in the Old Testament to be fulfilled in the New in the birth of our Lord and Saviour, Jesus Christ. Not only was His virgin birth foretold, but also the place of His nativity, for the prophet Micah is most explicit on this point: 'And thou Bethlehem—House of Ephratah, art few in number to be *reckoned* among the thousands of Judah; yet out of thee shall One come forth to Me, to be Ruler of Israel; and His goings forth were from the beginning, from eternity' (v. 2, Septuagint).

Some time before the incarnation of our Lord an opinion prevailed among the more pious Jews that Jehovah would condescend to favour them with a clearer revelation by the mission of some eminent person qualified from above to instruct them in the things pertaining to the Kingdom of God. This opinion was founded on the prediction of the ancient prophets, who had described with the utmost beauty and cleverness the person, character and glory of the Messiah.

Relying on the fulfilment of these prophecies, the devout persons amongst the Jews imagined the time appointed by God to be at hand, and that the promised Messiah would shortly make His appearance, and therefore are said to have waited night and day for 'the consolation of Israel.' A mighty Deliverer, a conquering Saviour, was their conception of what the first Advent should be and as a result very few of these watchers recognised in the child

Jesus, born of a Virgin, and in some obscurity, the fulfilment of the very prophecies on which they relied.

Today the virgin birth of Christ is generally accepted, yet there is a modern tendency to reject this great fundamental of the Christian Faith, upon which one theologian has written warningly: 'It is well known that the last ten or twenty years have been marked by a determined assault upon the truth of the virgin birth of Christ. ... because it is supposed that the evidence for this miracle is more readily got rid of than the evidence for public facts such as the resurrection. The result is that in very many quarters the virgin birth of Christ is treated as a fable.... Among those who reject the virgin birth of Christ the Lord, few will be found—I do not know any—who take, in other respects, an adequate view of the Person and work of the Saviour. ... Rejection of the virgin birth seldom, if ever, goes by itself. Those who take the lines of denial. ... do great injustice to the evidence and importance of the doctrine they reject. The evidence, if not of the same public kind as that for the resurrection, is far stronger than the objector allows, and the fact denied enters far more vitally into the essence of the Christian faith than he supposes. It is in truth a very superficial way of speaking or thinking of the virgin birth to say that nothing depends on this belief for our estimate of Christ. Who that reflects on the subject can fail to see that if Christ was virgin born—if He was truly conceived as the creed says, 'by the Holy Ghost, born of the Virgin Mary'—there must of necessity enter a supernatural element into His Person: while if Christ was sinless, much more if He was the Word of God incarnate, there must have been a miracle—the most stupendous miracle in the Universe—in His origin.

'One's mind turns first to that oldest of all evangelical promises that the seed of the woman would bruise the head of the serpent. "I will put enmity," says Jehovah to the serpent-tempter, "between thee and the woman, and between thy seed and her seed; it shall bruise thy head, and thou shalt bruise his heel." It is a forceless weakening of this first word of Gospel in the Bible to explain it as a lasting feud between the race of men and the brood of serpents. . . . The "Seed," who should destroy him is described emphatically as the woman's seed. . . . It remains significant that this peculiar phrase should be chosen to designate the future Deliverer. . . .

'By general consent the narrative in *Matthew* (ch. 1, 2) and in *Luke* (ch. 1, 2) are independent—that is they are not derived one from the other—yet they both affirm in detailed story that Jesus, conceived of the Holy Spirit, was born of a pure virgin, Mary of Nazareth, espoused to Joseph whose wife she afterwards became, a perusal of the narratives shows clearly—what might have been expected —that the information they convey was derived from no lower source than Mary and Joseph themselves. There is a marked feature of contrasts in the narratives—that Matthew's narrative is all told from Joseph's point of view, and Luke's is all told from Mary's. The signs of this are unmistakable. Matthew's tells about Joseph's difficulties and action, and says little or nothing about Mary's thoughts and feelings. Luke tells much about Mary—even her inmost thoughts—but says next to nothing directly about Joseph. The narratives are not contradictory, but are independent and complementary. The one supplements and complements the other. Both together are needed to give the whole story. They bear in themselves the stamp of truth, honesty and purity and are worthy of all acceptation.'[48]

The Virgin, being ordained by the Most High to be the mother of the Redeemer of Israel and the Saviour of the World, was saluted by the angel in language becoming her lofty destiny, 'Hail,

---

[48] Prof. James Orr, *The Fundamentals*, Vol. I.

thou that art highly favoured, the Lord is with thee.' Perceiving the goodness of her heart the angel vouchsafed an immediate answer to her enquiry as to how this could be brought about, 'The Holy Ghost shall come upon thee, and the power of the Highest shall overshadow thee,' or in other words, this marvellous event shall be brought about by the aid of the Holy Spirit and wonderful exertion of the power of the most High. 'And the angel said unto her. . . . Therefore also that holy thing which shall be born of thee shall be called the Son of God.'

It has been rightly pointed out that 'Mary had a wonderful character which is not sufficiently appreciated. She had reached that high pinnacle of purity and self-renunciation from which she could regard dishonour with scorn and allying her will with the will of her God she became in her own person the one to realise the promise that the Seed of the woman should bruise the serpent's head.' The self-dedication of Mary is emphasized in the marginal reading of *Luke* 1:28 (A.V.), where for 'highly favoured' we read 'graciously accepted.' Thus Mary believed unhesitatingly the announcement of the angel, 'The Lord God shall give unto Him the throne of His father David: and He shall reign over the house of Jacob for ever; and of His kingdom there shall be no end.'

When the Virgin realized that she was indeed to become a mother, to be blessed above women, for she, with the rest of the daughters of Israel had grown up with the hope of being selected by God to be the honoured mother of the Redeemer of Israel, she arose and went 'with haste' far away from Nazareth to a city of Judah, perhaps more correctly the city Judah in Judea, a Levitical city, ninety miles from Nazareth, to the house of her cousin Elizabeth, the wife of a high-standing priest there, Zacharias, both of them descendants of Aaron.

Upon reaching her cousin's house, where she abode three

months, Mary's joy was expressed in the beautiful song of the Magnificat:

'My soul doth magnify the Lord.

And my spirit hath rejoiced in God my Saviour.

For He hath regarded the low estate of His handmaiden:

For, behold, from henceforth all generations shall call me blessed.

For He that is mighty hath done to me great things; and holy is His name.

And His mercy is on them that fear Him from generation to generation.

He hath shewed strength with His arm; He hath scattered the proud in the imagination of their hearts.

He hath put down the mighty from their seats, and exalted them of low degree.

He hath filled the hungry with good things; and the rich He hath sent empty away.

He hath holpen His servant Israel, in remembrance of His mercy.

As He spake to our fathers, to Abraham, and to his seed forever.'

These deathless words of the blessed Virgin have been the comfort and joy of Christians for countless generations and in every clime.

Joseph, by Divine command, now became the husband and protector of Mary. 'Fear not to take unto thee Mary thy wife' and so together they went up to Bethlehem, 'the City of David,' to be taxed or enrolled according to the decree of Caesar Augustus that 'all the world should be taxed,' i.e. the Roman world.

The word translated 'inn' in *Luke* 1:7 as the place in which Mary and Joseph could not find shelter was not a 'khan' but a private dwelling house so full of guests at the time that hospitality could not be shown to Mary and her husband,[49] and so our Lord was born in one of the outbuildings and 'laid in a manger.' This, however, was a temporary measure for when the 'wise men from the East' arrived in Bethlehem they found Mary and her Divine Child 'in the house.' This house was, possibly, the 'House of Ephratah,' the ancestral home of David. Both Mary and Joseph were of the House and lineage of David: Mary through Nathan, and Joseph through Solomon, the sons of David by Bathsheba, his beloved wife.

Immediately after the departure of the 'Wise Men' Joseph was warned of God in a dream to take the young child and His mother and flee into Egypt in order to escape the ruthless slaying of young children by Herod, and there they remained until after the death of Herod, when was fulfilled the final event in a great national prophecy: 'Out of Egypt have I called My Son.' This is the last occasion on record upon which Egypt was used as a place of refuge for an Israelite.

At the three great feasts of the year when the Jews flocked into Jerusalem, it was the custom for afternoon lectures to be delivered in the Temple by the learned Rabbis of the day. It was encumbent upon the Jew to remain but three or four days at the seven days' Feast. Mary, with her husband, began the return journey to Nazareth as soon as they had performed those acts of worship required of them on these occasions. She believed her Son to be travelling in one of the companies of their relatives who had come up to the Feast. When at the first stopping place, Arimathea, eight miles north of Jerusalem, she could not find her young Son among any of these companies of their relatives, Mary, accompanied by Joseph, anxiously retraced her steps to Jerusalem, and after a three

---

[49] Geikie, *Life and Words of Christ*, Vol. I, p. 113.

days' search found Him in the Temple attending one of the lectures, and with His questions and answers confounding the learned professors. When gently rebuked, He replied in some astonishment, 'How is it that ye sought Me? wist ye not that I must be about My Father's business?' In His later years, during His three years' ministry He stated specifically what that business was: 'I am not sent but unto the lost sheep of the house of Israel.'

The next scriptural notice of the Virgin Mother is on the occasion of the marriage at Cana of Galilee, Mary interested herself in the conduct of the feast at which there happened to be a scarcity of wine. Representing to her Son, also a guest at the feast, that they had no wine, He gently replied, 'Woman, what have I to do with thee? Mine hour is not yet come,' that is, the time or period of His public ministry had not yet arrived, nor was it time yet for Him to exercise His powers in public. These words were not a rebuke to His mother, they were simply an explanation why He had not, without being asked, miraculously brought about a supply of wine. Mary's injunction to the servants, 'Whatsoever He saith unto you, do it,' was followed immediately by beholding her Divine Son perform His first public miracle.

There can be no doubt that the Virgin Mother was an onlooker at many of the miracles performed by our Lord, although, indeed, there is little mention of her in the Scripture records until we find her standing with her sister, the wife of Cleophas, and Mary Magdalene at some distance from the Cross, when the prophecy of Simeon was fulfilled, 'Yea, a sword shall pierce through thy own soul.'

When the sufferings of our Lord were almost at an end and the veil of darkness began to extend over the face of nature, they, with the beloved disciple, St. John, drew near to the foot of the Cross. Our Lord, beholding His mother and her companions, was greatly affected by their grief, especially that of His mother. He said, 'Woman, behold thy son!' and to St. John, 'Behold, thy mother!' The disciple immediately took her into his charge by leading her away from the dreadful scene to his own home, where he left her in the loving care of his family while he returned to the scene of the Crucifixion to be a witness of the last act in the cruel drama, and so was enabled to write, 'And he that saw it bare record, and his record is true: and he knoweth that he saith true, that ye might believe.'

It was surely an honour which our Lord conferred upon St. John by committing to his trust and care His sorrowful and disconsolate mother.

St. Luke gives many details not found in the other three Gospels: this is to be accounted for by the fact that this Apostle became a special friend and confidant of the Virgin Mary, who evidently told him secrets of her life which were hidden from the other evangelists.

In considering whether or not the Virgin Mother had other children after the birth of our Lord, there are several facts to lead us entirely away from this idea.

If our Lord had had blood brothers He could not, and would not, as a strict observer of the Mosaic law have committed His mother to the care of St. John for, according to that law, this duty was the responsibility of the next eldest son: neither, by the same law, could Joseph of Arimathea have obtained the body of our Lord; the brother next in succession must make the claim. Thus Joseph of Arimathea, his mother's uncle, was proclaimed for all time our Lord's nearest male relative.

Joseph, by his marriage to Mary, became the protector of both herself and her Son, and stood to our Lord legally in place of an earthly father; he was known locally as such and his children by a former wife were known as our Lord's 'brothers and sisters.' We must remember also that in those days 'brethren' was a very wide term, and if we made incursion into the realm of tradition we would find support for Mary having borne no other children.

'It is popularly conceived that Jesus, as the eldest of the family, had the numerous family of Joseph and Mary to support. This is all popular tradition, fostered by the Roman Catholic Church from its very beginning, but in reality does not contain one shred of factual truth.[50]

It is said that Mary, the mother of our Lord, lived at Jerusalem for fifteen years with St. John, and that this Apostle did not begin his missionary labours in Asia Minor until after her death and burial. Her grave is shown at Nazareth; it is said to be at the Mount of Olives; in the South of France, and at Glastonbury. Well it is that the burial place of the Virgin Mother is not known with any degree of certainty, for the Mariolatry which constitutes so great a menace to true Christianity would thereby be strengthened by pilgrimages to the spot, and in time obscure the sacrificial work of her Son, Jesus Christ: Son of God, Redeemer of Israel and Saviour of the World.

---

[50] J.O. Kinnaman, *Diggers for Facts*, p. 214.

CHAPTER 18

MARTHA AND MARY

Τ he historical background of the Bethany family is found in literature outside the Scriptures, yet none the less is it of special interest to those who have come to love the story of the sisters and their brother, whose devotion to our Lord is so beautifully portrayed for us in the Gospels.

According to the eighth century writer, Rabanus,[51] who based his work on earlier manuscripts and documents, Martha, Mary and their young brother Lazarus were of noble birth, their mother being Eucharia, descendant of the royal family of the House of David, and their father, Theophilus, a Syrian prince and Governor of the maritime country. These children were noted for their fine character and intelligence, and for their knowledge of the Hebrew language in which they had been well instructed. Martha is described as being much older than the other children.

They possessed a rich patrimony of lands, money and slaves; a great part of the city of Jerusalem belonged to them, also the village of Bethany, besides lands at Magdala (on the west side of the Lake of Galilee) and at another Bethany, or Bethabara.

The three lived together and Martha, as the eldest of the family, had the administration of their property. As the younger and beautiful sister, Mary, grew up she moved from Bethany and took up her residence at Magdala on her own property there, and it is said that there she lived a life of sin, in conscious disobedience to the command of God and to the wishes of her family until aroused

---

[51] *Life of Rabanus*, MS. in Magdalen College Library, Oxford.

by the preaching of our Lord and pardoned by Him in the house of Simon the Pharisee, where the first anointing took place immediately after her conversion. Simon is said to have been related to the Bethany family by 'ties of blood and of friendship.'

Another view of the history of Mary of Magdala or Mary Magdalene is that she had been insane. This view is based on the words 'out of whom went seven demons,' for there is no proof that she was ever impure in life. Whatever her malady 'her name stands security, as it were, for every penitent Magdalen.'

It was at Magdala at the estate of Mary Magdalene, that she with her sister Martha entertained our Lord and His disciples as recorded by *Luke* 10:38. In the company of Jesus were the twelve apostles, the seventy disciples and a large following of illustrious women, so it was natural that Martha, as the elder sister and chief hostess, should have been somewhat anxious about the preparation for so large a gathering. Marcella, stewardess of the house, a woman of great devotion and faith, together with Joanna and Susannah, assisted Martha in waiting on the guests. It is said that Marcella was the 'certain woman' of *Luke* 11:27.

At times our Lord is said to have used the other residences of the Bethany family, and that when He was gone on any distant journey and they could not accompany Him, refreshments and other necessities were sent to Him by the hands of the servants or by Judas Iscariot who had charge of the money and provisions.

According to a very old tradition Mary Magdalene was none other than Mary of Bethany, a tradition accepted by Tertullian, St. Ambrose, St. Jerome, St. Augustine, St. Gregory, the Venerable Bede, Rabanus, St. Odo, St. Bernard and St. Thomas Aquinas.

At the first anointing of Jesus' feet by Mary, Simon, in whose house the anointing took place, thought Jesus' admission to such familiarity, similar to that of affectionate daughters towards their father, was an evidence that He knew not her character or that she had been demon possessed and so, at one time, not responsible for her actions. Our Lord at once made it abundantly clear to Simon that Mary, by her works, was expressing her gratitude for forgiveness, while he, His host and supposed friend, had done nothing for Him, not even providing the customary basin of water to wash the dust of the journey from His feet. Mary's loving act was evidence that her sins were forgiven, but for the benefit of the onlookers He said to Mary 'Thy faith hath saved thee.'

Soon after, Mary is mentioned as one of Our Lord's ministering attendants.

The Bethany family found no difficulty in recognizing Jesus as the Messiah. The instruction in the Hebrew language which they had received in their early years was not without its thorough grounding in the Scriptures; they were not among those who preferred the Talmud and 'traditions of men' to the pure Word of God.

Mary's better part, or good part was to sit at the feet of Jesus and learn of Him; He was to her not only Lord but Master and Teacher. She sat at His feet as St. Paul, referring to his university days, states that he sat at the feet of Gamaliel, the learned Rabbinical professor.

St. John appears to have been a very special friend of the family and records (ch. 11) the greater part of what we know about them. He it is who tells us that 'Jesus loved Martha, and her sister, and Lazarus.'

And when Lazarus fell ill and rapidly grew worse, the sisters became alarmed and sent messengers to the place where Jesus then was—at Bethabara beyond Jordan, where Mary had her estate—with an urgent note: 'He whom Thou lovest is sick.'

There was no hurried return to Bethany as the sisters expected, and the beloved brother passed away ere the Lord came. Martha, confident of His sympathy, went out to meet Him when she heard of His approach. Mary, we are told, sat still in the house. Our Lord evidently enquired about her for Martha hurried back to say to Mary, 'The Master is come, and calleth for thee.'

The mournful utterances of both sisters, and their perfect confidence in the power of their Lord was expressed in the identical words: 'Lord, if Thou hadst been here my brother had not died.'

It was necessary for our Lord to have both sisters present to be witnesses of their brother's resurrection, to prepare them to expect His own resurrection after the soon-to-take-place Crucifixion.

But before Martha brought her sister, and, whilst in conversation with her Lord and Master, she made her wonderful affirmation of His Messiahship and power over life and death.

'Then said Martha unto Jesus, Lord, if Thou hadst been here, my brother had not died. But I know, that even now, whatsoever Thou wilt ask of God, God will give it Thee. Jesus saith unto her, Thy brother shall rise again. Martha saith unto Him, I know that he shall rise again in the resurrection at the last day. Jesus said unto her, I am the resurrection, and the life: he that believeth in Me, though he were dead, yet shall he live: and whosoever liveth and believeth in Me shall never die. Believest thou this? She saith unto him, Yea, Lord: I believe that Thou art the Christ, the Son of God, which should come into the world.'

No hint of our Lord's conversation with Mary is recorded, it is His words to Martha that have rung down the ages. She, the busy woman burdened with much care and responsibility, reveals her inner spiritual life in the simple words of her affirmation 'Lord I believe that Thou art the Christ, the Son of God.'

And now, in the raising of Lazarus from the dead, the sisters have a demonstration of the power of their Lord over life and death, as also the beloved brother restored to them. Another link had been forged in their chain of friendship, a link of deepest love and gratitude. Already they had stood loyally by Him in days of persecution; they loved to entertain Him and His disciples. How greatly they were the means of increasing His following by introducing their friends to Him, and now at the resurrection of their brother, Lazarus, many Jews believed on Him because of the astounding miracle.

It is a remarkable fact that the Bethany family had greater experience of resurrection than any other of our Lord's friends and followers.

With the happy family life restored the sisters were more than ever devoted to their Lord and Master; when next He came to Bethany they must entertain Him royally, and so we read that 'Jesus six days before the passover came to Bethany, where Lazarus was which had been dead, whom He raised from the dead. There they made Him a supper; and Martha served: but Lazarus was one of them that sat at the table with Him. Then took Mary a pound of ointment of spikenard, very costly, and anointed the feet of Jesus, and wiped His feet with her hair: and the house was filled with the odour of the ointment.'

This second anointing by Mary was again an act of gratitude—this time for the restoration to life of her brother. The ordinary anointing of hospitality was of the feet and head but Mary invested the anointing with the deeper meaning of the preparation of the body for burial, and the act was recognized and accepted by our Lord as such.

Mary attended our Lord on His last journey to Jerusalem, and witnessed His triumphal entry into Jerusalem on that first Palm Sunday. Five days later, with the deepest anguish, she witnessed

His crucifixion.

Early on the third day thereafter she and Mary, the wife of Cleophas, took the spices which they had prepared and went to the sepulchre to embalm the body—Joseph of Arimathea and Nicodemus having carried out the burial hastily with myrrh and aloes only, but finding His body gone an angel informed them that He was risen. As they were going to tell the disciples, Mary Magdalene returned and stood weeping at the sepulchre. There Jesus met her; she supposed He was the gardener, and asked Him if He knew what was become of her Lord's body that she might take care of it.

With His known air of speech, Jesus called her by her name. Recognizing Him immediately, she cried out in a rapture of joy, 'Rabboni,' which signifies 'Master,' and fell at His feet to embrace them, but He bade her forbear and go and inform His disciples that He was risen. As she went and overtook the other Mary, and other women, Jesus appeared to them. After this joyful reunion 'Mary Magdalene came and told the disciples that she had seen the Lord, and that He had spoken these things unto her.'

Beyond this meeting with Mary there is no Scripture reference to any member of the Bethany family after the Resurrection, but very credible tradition has it that in the persecution of Christians following upon the death of Stephen, these loved friends of our Lord, with other of His followers, were compelled to leave Palestine. According to a strong unvarying tradition to be found at many places along the coast of the Mediterranean, Lazarus, with some of his friends, came to Cyprus where he became the island's first missionary bishop, but afterwards sailed to Marseilles where he continued his missionary labours until his death.

Martha, according to the same tradition, came to Marseilles, accompanied by her stewardess, Marcella, and other early

Christians. She travelled up the Rhone valley to Tarascon where she and her companions settled and spent many years in missionary work.

Mary, with some of the less-known disciples, proceeded to Aix where she lived a life of extreme abstemiousness and laboured successfully for the Gospel of Jesus Christ.

The sisters, it is said, possessed 'a noble beauty, an honourable bearing, and a ready grace in language that was captivating.'

Martha's age at her death is given as sixty-five; the sisters died within eight days of each other.

The tradition of Martha at Tarascon, and Mary at Aix, dominates both town and church, while at Marseilles the memory of Lazarus has never died out.

We first meet this little family in the East; we bid them farewell in the West. They were but a part of that great East-West movement which brought the Gospel to our own shores from whence it has gone out to all the ends of the earth.

CHAPTER 19

THE WOMEN OF GALILEE

Against a background of much opposition to our Lord and His Gospel, there stands out the story of the courageous devotion of the women of Galilee, as recorded by the four Evangelists. The names of but a few of these women have come down to us.

It is necessary to have a proper understanding of the term Galilee, as distinct from the neighbouring Judea. Galilee was Benjamite territory, while the latter was inhabited by the descendants of Judah, more correctly a remnant of Judah. There was, far to the north, another Galilee, known as Galilee of the Gentiles because of the cosmopolitan character of its inhabitants and where Greek was the chief language. The people of lower Galilee and of Judea differed considerably in political outlook and even in speech, as borne out in the words of the bystanders to St. Peter, 'Surely thou art often of them: for thou art a Galilean, and thy speech agreeth thereto' *(Mark* 14:70). This was, of course, difference of accent, for all spoke the Aramaic language and in religion all were Hebrews and strict observers of the Mosaic law.

In Galilee our Lord had a large following: His disciples, with the possible exception of Judas Iscariot, were Galileans. In Judea He was persecuted and rejected; in Galilee He had a host of friends, many of them rich and influential. On one occasion while in Galilee His disciples expostulated with Him because He proposed to go again into Judea, saying 'Master, the Jews of late sought to stone Thee; and goest Thou thither again?' *(John* 11:8). It was in

Judea only that our Lord had not where to lay His head. In Galilee, and also when He went up to Jerusalem a little group of women followed from place to place devotedly ministering to His needs.

'They are first mentioned clearly in *Luke* 8:2, 3, as "Mary, called Magdalene . . . Joanna the wife of Chuza, Herod's steward, Susanna and many others." Those that are mentioned by name are probably the women of comfortable means "who ministered unto Him of their substance." Three of the "many others" can be identified, "Mary the mother of James and Joses; and the mother of Zebedee's children" (whose children were James and John, and the mother's name Salome): and the mother of Jesus, frequently mentioned. . . . From the expression "many others" we infer that the number of women who accompanied Jesus in His three years' ministry was not inconsiderable. They must have witnessed most of His miracles: heard most of His discourses, seen His sufferings, and known His claims—that He was the Messiah. These women had no more lofty ambition for themselves than to minister unto their Lord. To be sure, the mother of Zebedee's children, the aunt of Jesus Christ, is shown as asking for a high place for her sons in Christ's kingdom: but it is evident that she was pressed into this service by her sons—since the Lord answers, not her, but the sons, "Ye know not what ye ask;" and "When the ten heard it they were moved with indignation against the brethren." This shows that they did not hold the mother culpable. Mark does not even mention the mother as voicing the request of the sons. No, these women who followed the Lord had no wishes of their own to be gratified. Their service was a disinterested one.'[52]

The women of Galilee accompanied our Lord on His last journey to Jerusalem. They followed Him weeping, whereupon He turned and addressed them, 'Daughters of Jerusalem, weep not for

---

[52] Katharine Bushnell, *God's Word to Women*, paras. 742-757.

Me, but weep for yourselves.' Our Lord here used a very precise geographical term, for Jerusalem was in Benjamin's inheritance and so these Galilean women were strictly 'daughters of Jerusalem.' They followed Him to Calvary; they remained to witness the tragedy of the Cross: when all was over, yet they lingered; and when the body was laid in the tomb 'The women also, which came with Him from Galilee, followed after, and beheld the sepulchre, and how His body was laid.' Evening came on, the last service to the dead body was performed, the stone closed over the tomb, but yet 'there was Mary Magdalene, and the other Mary, sitting over against the sepulchre.' The question might be asked. Did Jesus have no higher choice for the women who came with Him out of Galilee, and accompanied Him throughout His three years' ministry—the women who were "last at the Cross and first at the tomb" on the Resurrection morn—than to let them feed and clothe Him? Were they not all unconsciously to themselves in a school of training as His witnesses? His twelve apostles called for this special work all, but one, failed Him, when danger was at hand. But He had His chosen witnesses: the women of Galilee. They had humbled themselves; Christ exalted them. He gave them visions on the Resurrection morning that no one else had. He made the witness of women the very meat and marrow of His Gospel.'[53]

After our Lord's ascension a remarkable feature of these earliest Christian women was the jealous way in which they guarded the bodies of their dead. 'They had seen the Lord after He had risen from the dead, and must have been at first uncertain as to what might be expected regarding the bodies of those they loved, and especially the bodies of those who had died for the Faith. Until this could be certain they hoped against hope for those whom they

---

[53] ibid, para. 758.

had loved and honoured and revered, that some morning the lifeless clay might have vanished from its resting place, and the risen master, or father or son be waiting to greet the watching disciple.'[54]

The dislike of the earliest Christians for burial in pagan cemeteries is thus easily understood: the setting apart of ground to receive the bodies of those who had died in the Lord gave rise to the idea of a hallowed enclosure which persists to this day in the term 'consecrated ground.'

The Prophet Joel declared, 'Your daughters shall prophesy . . . and on my handmaidens I will pour out in those days of My Spirit; and they shall prophesy' *(Acts* 2:17, 18). The women of Galilee were thus spiritually equipped to be witnesses and messengers of the Gospel and to fulfil the prophecy of Isaiah, 'Oh thou woman,[55] that bringest good tidings to Zion, get thee up into the high mountain; Oh thou woman that bringest good tiding to Jerusalem, lift up thy voice with strength; lift it up, be not afraid; say unto the cities of Judah, Behold your God!' *(Isaiah* 40:9)—a command which will find its final fulfilment as a great prophecy towards the end of the Gospel Dispensation.

---

[54] J.W. Taylor, *The Coming of the Saints*, p. 221.
[55] Author's Note—This is the precise meaning if correctly translated.

CHAPTER 20

DORCAS (*Acts* 9:36-42)

In the earliest days of the Church there dwelt at Joppa, now Jaffa, a much beloved Christian woman whose name, Dorcas, was the Greek form of the Aramaic Tabitha, signifying 'gazelle' because of the animal's large eyes, a woman venerable for her piety and extensive charity.

Dorcas possessed the faith, humility, diligence and perseverance of the true disciple. Widows, being the poorest and most helpless in the community, were the chief objects of her charity. 'This woman was full of good works and almsdeeds which she did,' or charities to the poor. Latimer wrote, 'He loveth thee with his hands that will help thee in time of necessity by giving some almsdeeds, or with any other occupation of the hands.' When this loved benefactor sickened and died they were filled with sorrow and dismay.

The last offices had been performed and Dorcas laid 'in an upper chamber.' Then with that faith in the power of the risen Christ which marked the early disciples, and having heard that Peter was at Lydda, twelve miles away, 'they sent unto him two men, desiring him that he would not delay to come to them. Then Peter arose and went with them. When he was come, they brought him into the upper chamber: and all the widows stood by him weeping, and shewing the coats and garments which Dorcas made, while she was with them.'

The mourners, wearing the garments which Dorcas had made, sought to impress St. Peter with the value of her life to them. 'But

Peter put them all forth, and kneeled down, and prayed; and turning him to the body said, Tabitha, arise. And she opened her eyes: and when she saw Peter, she sat up. And he gave her his hand, and lifted her up, and when she had called the saints and widows, presented her alive. And it was known throughout all Joppa; and many believed in the Lord.'

On this miracle St. Cyprian in the third century wrote, 'She, who to suffering widows had dispensed the means of living, earned a recall to life through the widows' intercession.'

Life returned to Dorcas without violent emotion, calmly, as to one awakened out of sleep, to resume her good works and to continue her witness for her Lord and Saviour Jesus Christ.

The restoration to life of Dorcas was an unspeakable benefit to the world. So wonderful an event was soon widely published and many believed in the Lord. The good work of this saintly woman was taken up as a challenge by Christian women throughout the centuries and the name 'Dorcas' given to guilds and societies which had as their object the making of garments for the poor. A small charge was made in cases of ability to pay but the very poor were ever provided with garments free of charge.

The site of the house in which Dorcas lived, and her tomb, are still shown as among the sights of Jaffa.

CHAPTER 21

LYDIA *(Acts* 16:8-15)

The scene by the riverside at Philippi in Macedonia on the Sabbath morning was one of peace and quietness even if nearby there was all the bustle and activity of a Roman Colony. A *Colonia* was Rome transplanted, and these colonies were primarily intended as military safeguards of the frontiers. The colonists went out with all the pride of Roman citizens to represent and reproduce the city in the midst of an alien population.

Here, in Philippi, St. Paul found himself in obedience to the voice of the vision at Troas, 'Come over into Macedonia and help us,' and a more uncongenial or unlikely field for the preaching of the Gospel it would have been difficult to find.

By the riverside there was a quiet spot, a retreat known to the Jews, where they could assemble unmolested and 'where prayer was wont to be made,' there being no synagogue in the place. Here, one Sabbath morning, as St. Paul was proceeding along the river-bank to join the little company, he 'sat down, and spake unto the women which resorted thither.'

Among them there was a woman of Thyatira, who had come to Philippi in connection with her business as 'a seller of purple,' that is a seller of fabrics dyed purple. Those engaged in this business were known as Lydians, from Lydia, the country where the fabrics were woven and dyed, the inhabitants being famed for this industry. The art of dyeing is still practised in the modern town, called Akhissar. When St. Paul began to explain the way of salvation, this woman known to us as Lydia, indifferent and self-satisfied, heard the eloquent words of the Apostle as he delivered his great message of the Gospel, and as she listened conviction began to steal upon her 'whose heart the Lord opened, that she attended unto the things which were spoken of Paul.' Lydia is described as one who 'worshipped God,' therefore she was not a pagan, but probably a Jewess or one of the Greek-speaking Israelites who at that time were domiciled in Asia Minor.

The consequence of the opening of her heart was an earnest attention to the Word: a public profession of her faith and the baptism of herself and her household. Immediately afterwards there was the manifestation of a self-sacrificing spirit: 'She besought us, saying, If ye have judged me to be faithful to the Lord, come into my house, and abide there. And she constrained us.' Lydia modestly desires this to be decided for her by others. Henceforth St. Paul and his companions were the welcome guests of Lydia when they came to Philippi; a home provided for them in a strange city as the result of the conversion of Lydia; and to the house of Lydia Paul and Silas resorted upon their release from prison (v. 40).

In the history of the primitive advance of Christianity the name of Dorcas is outstanding as an example in charitable deeds, while that of Lydia is outstanding as an example of that hospitality which ever marks the true Christian. In the *Acts of the Apostles* their names are recorded as worthy of remembrance by future generations.

CHAPTER 22

PRISCILLA *(Acts* 18:1, 2, 26)

W hen the Apostle Paul arrived in Corinth from Athens he 'found a certain Jew named Aquila, born in Pontus, lately come from Italy, with his wife Priscilla (because that Claudius had commanded all Jews to depart from Rome) and came unto them.' It would appear from the wording of the text that Aquila and Priscilla were old friends of St. Paul. He 'found' them there and immediately took up his abode with them. They had already become converts to Christianity before St. Paul met with them at Corinth.

According to a very strict law every Jew was obliged to learn a trade: the professional classes were not exempt from this, and to be able to earn a living with work of the hands was viewed as security against poverty. The trade chosen by the highly-educated St. Paul was that of tent-making, which was also the trade of his friend, Aquila. Their work, that of making leather tents for the Roman troops, was skilled labour, and in much demand. Some of our Lord's disciples appear to have been scribes, while fishing was merely their chosen trade, for when He spoke to them in parables and then asked them, 'Have ye understood all these things? They say unto Him, Yea, Lord,' it is as scribes that He then addresses them: 'Therefore every scribe which is instructed unto the kingdom of heaven is like unto a man that is an householder, which bringeth forth out of his treasure things new and old' *(Matthew* 13: 5-52).

The co-operation in crafts, as also in missionary work, created between St. Paul, Aquila and Priscilla a strong bond of friendship, the latter being especially helpful to the Apostle.

Priscilla was a very able person and well known 'to all the churches of the Gentiles;' she it was who, with her husband, Aquila, expounded unto Apollos 'the way of God more perfectly.' Dean Alford, in his *Commentary on the New Testament,* says, 'There are certain indications that he himself (Aquila) was rather the ready and zealous patron than the teacher: and this latter work, or a great share of it, belonged to his wife, Prisca or Priscilla. She is ever named with him even where the instruction of Apollos is described.'

On Priscilla's position, in *The Apostolic Church,* Professor Harnack says: 'In any case she must have been associated with and more distinguished than her husband. This is verified from *Acts* 18 and *Romans* 16 convincingly. For according to the former not only Aquila but she also instructed Apollos. One is allowed to infer from it that she was the chief instructor: otherwise she would scarcely have been mentioned. And in the Roman Epistle St. Paul calls her and Aquila—not the latter only—his fellow labourers in Christ Jesus. This expression, not so very frequently employed by Paul, signifies much.' By its use Priscilla and Aquila are legitimized official Evangelists and Teachers. Paul adds, moreover, the following: 'Who for my life laid down their own necks: unto whom not only I give thanks, but also all the churches of the Gentiles.' To what heroic service the first half of this clause refers we unfortunately know not. From the second part it follows that the Christian activity of the couple was a genuinely ecumenical work. Why all the Churches of the Gentiles were obliged to thank Priscilla and Aquila St. Paul does not say. Dr. Harnack adds in a footnote, quoting the views of Origen and Chrysostom as in accord with his own, 'That the thanks of the Gentile Churches relate only to the fact that Priscilla and Aquila saved the life of the Apostle is to me not probable.'

In the appalling persecution and martyrdom which befell the Christians through Nero's ferocity St. Paul lost many of his friends and fellow helpers named by him in the sixteenth chapter of *Romans*. That Priscilla escaped martyrdom is certain from the Apostle's mention of her name in his second *Epistle to Timothy,* chapter 4, verse 19.

Priscilla is worthy of grateful remembrance by the entire Christian Church for the devoted and sacrificial assistance she rendered the great Apostle as his hostess, fellow worker and 'helper in Christ.'

In the reign of Domitian (AD 81-96), Juvenal records a great and wealthy Jewish colony on Mount Aventine where was the house of Aquila and Priscilla, and where St. Paul ministered to the Christian Jew-converts who would not mix with the Christian Gentiles.

Dr. Harnack, a German writer, says that in Rome Priscilla, with the help of Aquila, wrote the *Epistle to the Hebrews*.

CHAPTER 23

THE MOTHER OF ST. PAUL

The Apostle Paul, in his letter to the Romans (ch. 16), sends salutations to a number of Christians and kinsfolk in that city including 'Rufus chosen in the Lord, and his mother and mine.'

Behind this simple message there lies a wealth of family history unrecorded in the Scriptures, but found from unpublished sources and tradition and published by Edwin Wilmshurst in his *St. Paul in Britain*. Two special journeys to Rome and one to Jerusalem enabled this writer to discover much that is of the highest importance and interest.

The grandfather of Saul (Paul) was a very wealthy Benjamite of Tarsus, capital of Gilicia, the rocky province in Asia Minor, due north of Syria. Romano-Graeco Hebrew, he had purchased 'with a great sum' the Roman citizenship for himself and family, and had added a Roman name to his Hebrew patronymic. His son, Davidus, as was usual, added a Roman nomen—Appius Tullius—being possibly adopted into the Tullian Gens. He took service in the Roman army; rose to be a centurion in a legion; and it was he who said to the Christ 'speak the word only and my servant shall be healed.' Of him the Jews said, 'He hath built us a synagogue,' an act inexplicable if the Romanized centurion had had no interest in the scorned religion of the Jews. His wife, Prassede, was left a wealthy widow, cultured by a Roman education. Pudentinus the Patrician was in Asia Minor on civil (not military) duty as a high Roman official, and he married the widow Prassede, a marriage probably very displeasing to her son Saul, who was an ultra-orthodox and intolerant Pharisee, of the strictest sect of their religion, and who assumed the Roman name of Paulus. Pudentinus and his wife, Prassede, returned to Italy, and one child, Rufus Pudens, was born to them. Saul, highly educated in the school of Gamaliel, the most orthodox in Jerusalem, was a fierce and uncompromising opponent of the sect of the Nazarenes, and his wealth and social position among the Jews was so high that he was entrusted by the High Priest with the mission to Damascus, with a military escort, to extirpate the heresy in that city.

Many wealthy Jews took service in the Roman army: it is not surprising then that Saul's father, Davidus of Tarsus, was either destined for that career by his father, or embarked upon it of his own volition.

That he was early impressed, while a centurion at Capernaum, with the claims of our Lord to be the Messiah, and also beloved of his countrymen, the Jews, for his generosity ('He hath built us a synagogue'), is evident from the Scripture narrative.

It was a common practice among the inhabitants of Tarsus to send their children into other cities for learning and improvement, especially to Jerusalem, where they were so numerous that they had a synagogue of their own, called the synagogue of the Cilicians. To Jerusalem Davidus, the centurion, sent his son Saul (Paul) to be brought up at the feet of the eminent Rabbi, Gamaliel, in the most exact knowledge of the law of Moses. It was common for the descendants of Benjamin to give the name of Saul to their children ever since the time of the first king of Israel, who was chosen out of that tribe, and Paul was a name common among the Romans.

When Davidus, the centurion, met his son at Jerusalem or when home on leave at Tarsus, he did not hesitate to declare his belief in Jesus of Nazareth as the long-expected Messiah Who had miraculously healed his servant. The centurion's wife, Prassede, quickly grasped the truth and became a convert, but their son Saul would have none of it. Having obtained a thorough knowledge of the sciences cultivated by the Jews, and being naturally of a hot and fiery temper, he became impatient of any opposition to the doctrine he had imbibed, and a vehement blasphemer and persecutor of the Christians. Had not the Pharisees declared that Jesus of Nazareth was not the Messiah? Did not he himself know that his nation expected their king to come in majesty and power?

Saul's father, Davidus, died, leaving his son quite unconvinced of the truth of this New Way. Now that his father was gone he would try by every means in his power to destroy this new religion: his social rank and wealth enabled him to approach the Sanhedrin with suggestions to this end, and from the High Priest he obtained letters of authority to proceed to Damascus to exterminate the Christians who had fled there for safety. Saul was provided with a military escort and set out on the long journey of 150 miles.

As he rode along he began to feel less zeal for this malicious enterprise. What if, after all, his father was right? He had been so certain that Jesus of Nazareth was the Christ and Saul had noticed a change in his father's demeanour, a gracious tolerance and spirit of love towards those with whom he came in contact. And his sweet and gentle mother, was she, too, really deceived? But he would put these uncomfortable thoughts from him; his conscience was getting troublesome: soon now he would reach Damascus and do away with these Christians who dared to say that the Sanhedrin was in error in rejecting Jesus of Nazareth. And then again his conscience became uneasy: the incidents of his father's last illness and the pained expression on his mother's face at his attitude to this New Way rose up before him. And then there was Stephen, to whose death he had consented, with forgiveness on the martyr's lips and holy confidence in God, breathing out his last words 'Lord Jesus, receive my spirit.' But why did his conscience prick him so? He was surely in the right to get rid of these Christians.

Such were Saul's thoughts as he was about to enter Damascus when 'suddenly there shined round about him a light from heaven: and he fell to the earth, and heard a voice saying unto him, Saul, Saul, why persecutest thou Me? And he said, Who art thou, Lord? And the Lord said, I am Jesus whom thou persecutest: it is hard for thee to kick against the pricks. And he trembling and astonished said, Lord, what wilt thou have me to do? And the Lord, said unto him, Arise, and go into the city, and it shall be told thee what thou must do. And the men which journeyed with him stood speechless, hearing a voice, but seeing no man. And Saul arose from the earth; and when his eyes were opened, he saw no man: but they led him by the hand, and brought him into Damascus. And he was three days without sight, and neither did eat nor drink. And there was a certain disciple at Damascus, named Ananias; and to him said the Lord in a vision, Ananias. And he said, Behold, I am here, Lord. And the Lord said unto him, Arise, and go into the street which is called Straight, and enquire in the house of Judas for one called Saul, of Tarsus: for, behold, he prayeth, and hath seen in a vision a man named Ananias coming in, and putting his hand on him, that he might receive his sight. Then Ananias answered, Lord, I have heard by many of this man, how much evil he hath done to thy saints at Jerusalem. And here he hath authority from the chief priests to bind all that call on Thy name. But the Lord said unto him, Go thy way: for he is a chosen vessel unto Me, to bear My name before the Gentiles, and kings, and the children of Israel: for I will shew him how great things he must suffer for My name's sake' *(Acts* 9:3-16).

The conversion of St. Paul is perhaps the most dramatic incident in the Apostolic Church, and with what joy his mother, Prassede, heard of the great change which had taken place in her son.

Saul had probably never seen his half-brother, Rufus Pudens, and certainly had never visited his mother in Rome before his conversion, but after then, in his letter to the Romans (ch. 16), he writes, 'Salute Rufus,' calling him by his domestic and family name, 'and his mother and mine.'

It is a remarkable fact that Prassede's two sons are the only two persons mentioned in the New Testament of whom the term 'chosen' is specially used. The mother of St. Paul was at hand to comfort and encourage him during his imprisonment in Rome. Of both her sons, Prassede must have been justly proud: her elder son 'a chosen vessel unto the Lord;' the younger son, named by St. Paul as 'chosen' in the Lord, who, by his gifts and endowments, did so much for the early Christian Church.

The sister of Prassede, Saul's mother, was named Mariamne but upon marriage with another Roman patrician she assumed the name of Priscilla. She also was left a rich widow, was converted, and on her own property outside the Salarian Gate, as was the custom, she constructed a private cemetery, still known as the Catacomb of Priscilla. Both sisters were members of an illustrious group of Christians in Rome, many of whom were martyred for their faith in Christ. The great Apostle was ever upheld by their prayers and loving sympathy and not least by Prassede, his mother, nor was she least among the women of Israel.

CHAPTER 24

CLAUDIA (II *Timothy* 4:21)

T he fellow-helpers and friends of St. Paul are gratefully mentioned by the Apostle throughout his Epistles; in the absence of historical records the majority of these must remain mere names to the reader. Of one of these friends, however, Claudia, mentioned in the Apostle's charge to Timothy, there is a wealth of documentary evidence of her noble birth, her literary attainments and her support, with her husband, of the early Church.

The story, briefly told, begins in the early days of the Christian era in Britain, when Caractacus succeeded his father, Cunobeline, the British king (the Cymbeline of Shakespeare) and became Arviragus, or 'high king.' By both these appellations he was well known to the Romans.

Upon his succession, this warrior (now also Pendragon, or leader in war) continued the struggle against the invading Romans and scorned the offers of peace made by the Emperor, Claudius Caesar, who had landed in Britain with a fresh military contingent; his nobles, however, advised him to accept the offer of reconciliation made by Claudius: that of marriage with the Emperor's daughter (the Venissa of the Welsh records).[56] This marriage proved entirely happy and of the five children born to them, Claudia, so named after her grandfather, Claudius, was the eldest; the Roman name Claudia becomes Gladys in the Celtic language. It is said that Claudia received a Roman education under the personal supervision of the Emperor. There at Rome, in a later

---

[56] Geoffrey of Monmouth's *British History*, Ch. XV.

year, with her parents and brothers and sister, Claudia met the Apostle Paul and with them embraced the Christian faith, the New Way which was the subject of so much controversy and persecution.

On the return of the British royal family to Britain, Caractacus, the Arviragus, found that the peace treaty had been broken and that his people were again being harassed by the Roman Generals. In AD 51, after only eight years of peace, Caractacus was once more obliged to take up arms against the invader. Again his bravery was at once the admiration and fear of the Romans; the stern Chief was betrayed, not conquered, through the treachery of his step-mother, Cartismandua, and carried to Rome in triumph. His wife, Venus Julia, and his young daughter Claudia, accompanied him, and there before the Senate he delivered his eloquent and moving speech. Release was immediately granted on the condition that never again would he bear arms against Rome.[57]

On his return Arviragus encouraged and assisted those Britons who had become Christian, as also the persecuted Christians who had fled to these shores; of great practical assistance was the gift of twelve hides of land at Glastonbury, free of tax, on which was built the first Christian church in Britain. This land has never paid tax.[58] One hide of land was sufficient to support a household.

In AD 60, at the age of seventeen, Claudia was united in marriage with Rufus Pudens (who had been in Britain on military duty), son of Prassede and Pudentinus, and therefore half-brother to the Apostle Paul. Thereafter, Claudia was known as Claudia Rufina, the latter name to designate her as wife of Rufus Pudens—philosopher and member of the Equestrian Order.

From the Epigrams of the poet Martial, we find that about AD 60 Rufus Pudens, upon the death of his father, had succeeded to the

[57] British Chronicles.
[58] Domesday Survey, fol. p. 449.

ancestral estates; this writer records the Senator's marriage in Rome to the British Claudia. The poet extols her beauty, learning and eminent virtues:

'Claudia, the fair one from a foreign shore is with my Pudens bound in wedlock's band' and in a later Epigram, the poet writes:

'Our Claudia, named Rufina, sprung we know from blue-eyed Britons; yet behold she vies in grace with all that Greece or Rome can show, As born and bred beneath their glowing skies.'[59]

We learn from the Roman martyrology that Claudia wrote several volumes of odes and hymns; these were preserved at Verulam (St. Albans in Hertfordshire) down to the thirteenth century. Of the poetic writings of Claudia, Balaeus (AD 400), mentions a book of Epigrams: *Elegy on her Husband's Death,* and other verses.

Four children were born to Claudia and Rufus Pudens, named Timotheus and Novatus, sons, and Prassede and Pudentiana, daughters. All four suffered martyrdom for the Faith.[60]

From before the reign of Augustus Caesar, the Senatorial family of the Pudentini held a high position among the great patrician families of Rome. Their palatium, or town house, with its grounds and detached buildings, covered more than twenty acres on the crest of the Esquiline Mount, and four hundred slaves of both sexes, born on their ancestral estates in Umbria, formed a part of their numerous retinue.

When St. Paul came to Rome he was received as a relative and honoured guest at the Palatium of Claudia and Pudens, parts of which still remain perfect. The chamber in the basement of the detached building of the Palace where St. Paul officiated in the Christian services is shown under the present upper St. Pudentiana. The theologian, Alban Butler, calls it the oldest Church in Rome;

---

[59] Epigrams 32, 40.
[60] Roman Martyrology.

here is the earliest mosaic in Rome, in which are portraits of Claudia, Rufus Pudens and their four children.

St. Paul, on his release from custody, three days after his arrival in Rome, would be at home at once among his friends and relatives. From 'his own hired house,' which he was obliged to retain as a prisoner in free custody, the Apostle would often repair to the magnificent home of the British Claudia [61] —an ever-welcome guest, and it is even said that her children were brought up 'on the knees of the Apostle.'

It was in the home of Claudia that St. Paul wrote his last letter to Timothy, then at Ephesus, and conveys to his beloved fellow-worker the greetings of Claudia, her husband, Pudens, and her brothers, Eubulus and Linus—the latter the first Bishop of Rome (II *Timothy* 4:21).

Rufus Pudens was assassinated in AD 96. Claudia died in peace in Umbria about AD 100.

King Lucius, the grandson of Claudia and Rufus Pudens, in AD 155, at a National Council held at Winchester, established Christianity as the national religion instead of Druidism; in this royal family there began to be fulfilled the prophecy, 'Kings shall see and arise, princes also shall worship.' 'Kings shall be thy nursing fathers and their queens thy nursing mothers' *(Isaiah* 49:7, 23).

Claudia lived at a time when Christianity was beginning to influence the Judaizers, and those who would keep women in subjection, while in Asia Minor women were long since emancipated from pagan tyranny. Sir William Ramsay, in his *The Church in the Roman Empire,* says: 'The honours and influence which belonged to women in the cities of Asia Minor form one of the most remarkable features in the history of the country. In all

---

[61] It was the *hospitium* for Christians from all parts of the world.

periods the evidence runs on the same lines. On the border between fable and history we find the Amazons. Under the Roman Empire we find women magistrates, presidents at games and loaded with honours. The custom of the country influenced even the Jews, who, at least in one case appointed a woman at Smyrna to the position of "Ruler of the Synagogue".'

This emancipation was lost when, as Sir William Ramsay points out, the universal and catholic type of Christianity became confirmed in its dislike of the prominence and public ministrations of women.

Many centuries were to elapse ere woman was again in her rightful position; throughout these ages woman has paid the price and lived subject to the rule of man. Jesus Christ taught rules of life as God requires, not as man would have it, and for the first time in history women were given hope in this world and the next. This teaching was revolutionary considering the status of women at that time, and far-reaching in its effect upon her restoration to freedom, civil rights, abolition of injustices, and that equality which is her right by Divine decree.

BIBLIOGRAPHY

The Bible, Authorized and Revised Versions, Septuagint,
  Ferrar Fenton
Cruden's Concordance, People's Bible Encyclopaedia,
  Clarke's Commentary

Alford, Dean, *Commentary on the New Testament*
Balaeus (AD 400), quoted in Betham's *Celebrated Women*
British Chronicles
Bruce, James, *African Travels*
Bullinger, Dr. E.W., *Number in Scripture*
Bushnell, Katherine, *God's Word to Women*
Cable, Mildred, and Francesca French, *Through Jade Gates*
Cassell in Lance's *Commentary on Authorized Version*
Charles, R.H., D.D., D.Litt., *The Testaments of the Twelve
  Patriarchs*
Conder, C.R., *Handbook Palestine Fund Report*
Cooper, Duff, *David*
Cyprian, St., quoted in *Biblical Museum*
Dead Sea Scrolls
Domesday Survey
Geikie, Cunningham, *Life and Words of Christ*; *The Holy
  Land and the Bible*
Goard, Dr. W. Pascoe, *The Book of Esther*
Harnack, Theodosius, *The Apostolic Church*
Josephus, *Antiquities*
Juvenal
Kinnaman, J.O., *Diggers for Facts*
Lofts, N., *Women in the Old Testament*
Malcolm, Sir John, *Sketches on Persia*
Marston, Sir Charles, *The Bible Comes Alive*
Martial
Moigne, P. Le, in Betham's *Celebrated Women*

163

Monmouth, Geoffrey of, *British History*

Munroe, Rev. J. Inverach, M.A., *The Samaritan Pentateuch and Modern Criticism*

Orr, Prof. James, *The Fundamentals*, Vol. I

Ouseley, Sir George Gore, *Biblical Museum*

Payne-Smith, Robert, *Prophecy a Preparation for Christ*

Petrie, Sir Flinders, *Egypt and Israel*

Pliny

Polak, Dr. J.E., *Persia*

Porter, J.L., D.D., *The Giant Cities of Bashan*

Porter, Sir R.E., on Esther's Tomb

Rabanus, *Life of Rabanus*

Ramsay, Sir William, *The Church in the Roman Empire*

Roman Martyrology

Schroeder, *Commentary*

Smith, Prof. Robertson, *Kinship and Marriage in Early Arabia*

Stanley, Dean, *Sinai and Palestine*

Taylor, J.W., *The Coming of the Saints*

Upham, Prof., *Wise Men*

Wilmshurst, Edwin, *St. Paul in Britain*